Shadows of Sherman Institute
A Photographic History of the Indian School on Magnolia Avenue

Shadows of Sherman Institute
A Photographic History of the Indian School on Magnolia Avenue

By
Clifford E. Trafzer
Jeffrey Allen Smith
Lorene Sisquoc

GREAT OAK PRESS, PECHANGA, CALIFORNIA

Copyright © 2017 by Clifford E. Trafzer, Jeffrey Allen Smith, Lorene Sisquoc

A CIP catalog record for this book is available from the Library of Congress.

ISBN: 978-1-942279-13-6

Publisher: Great Oak Press, Pechanga, California

Printed in the United States of America

For Galen Townsend, Ida Gooday Largo, and Tonita Largo

For Sherman Students and Brats, Past and Present

For Lee Ann, Dani, and Billy

Dear Readers,

Pechanga established the Great Oak Press in order to provide an avenue by which Native voices and topics of significance and of importance to Native Americans could find their way into the contemporary discourse and become both a growing and permanent part of recorded knowledge.

As a publisher of scholarly and academic books, Pechanga's Great Oak Press is dedicated to working with the leading experts and also the up and coming experts in a wide range of fields, ranging from the arts to the sciences and from history to languages. Our focus, though broad in topics, is finely centered on publishing works of great importance that preserve and expand knowledge as well as encourage creative thought and intellectual exploration.

However, Great Oak Press is not focused solely on producing scholarly titles that only the academic and higher education community find accessible. Rather, Great Oak Press is committed to producing books of exceptional quality that literally begin with First Readers for children and will include works for the entire range that comprises the K-12 reading levels. After all, the health of society is directly related to its efforts at raising and educating its youth.

In this powerful work, Shadows of Sherman, the evolution of this landmark institution, the Sherman Indian High School, is presented through Lorene Sisquoc's unparalleled lens of understanding and knowledge of the long, storied history of Sherman. Since 1991, Lorene has been the Curator at the Sherman Indian Museum, while her association with Sherman goes back decades before her curatorship, as she was literally raised at Sherman by her mother Tonita Largo Glover and her grandma Ida Gooday Largo. Lorene's collaborators on this remarkable project are the esteemed Dr. Cliff Trafzer, Costo Professor of American Indian Studies at the University of California, Riverside and Dr. Jeffrey Smith of the University of Hawaii, Hilo. Together, the authors have culled remarkable archival images, stories and documents and with these, they have woven the history of Sherman that has never been available until now.

We thank you for your support.

Mark Macarro
Tribal Chairman of the Pechanga Band of Luiseño Indians

Contents

Preface

The Indian School on Magnolia Avenue played a significant part in American history, but most Americans know little about its place in the nation's past. Sherman Institute, one of the nation's off-reservation American Indian boarding schools created by the federal government, was a symbol of assimilation. Established in 1902, federal policy makers built Sherman and the other Indian schools to destroy Native American cultures, languages, religions, and economies. Acting to reform American Indian policies, federal officials and Christian reformers actively changed American Indian policy from one designed to kill Indians through war to pacify them through education. In 1902, the Office of Indian Education built Sherman as an educational institution devoted to destroying indigenous cultures by capturing and controlling through military actions and participated in a program to capture and control Native American children.

Sherman's existence stemmed from the national objective of assimilating Indians into the dominant society. Civilization and Christianization of American Indian children became a major project of the federal government, and taxpayers provided millions of dollars to remake Native American children into useful laborers and contributing members of the United States. Policy makers had little hope to change adult and elder indigenous people. Instead, reformers removed children of all ages from their parents, homes, and communities to incarcerate them in off-reservation boarding schools where they could dominate and control most aspects of young lives. Sherman Institute played an important role in this national experiment to bring indigenous people into the fabric of the United States and its market economy as civilized Christians and useful laborers.

Sherman Institute became a symbol of assimilation and transformation to American Indian students. But Sherman changed over time, eventually becoming an institution devoted to the preservation of Native American cultures, languages, and spiritual beliefs. For many years, the authors have enjoyed an association with Sherman Indian Museum, located in the old adobe Administration building of Sherman Institute. Lorene Sisquoc grew up at Sherman with other "Sherman Brats." Like other indigenous children whose parents and grandparents worked at Sherman, Sisquoc grew up on campus but could not attend Sherman. Like Galen Townsend and other Sherman Brats, the federal government prevented the children of Sherman employees from attending school at Sherman. Since childhood, Sisquoc attended school off the Sherman campus.

In the 1990s, Sisquoc volunteered her time and talents to preserving the history of the school through Sherman Indian Museum. Today, she is the Curator of the Museum, and she teaches cultural studies and public history. Sherman students and volunteers work with Sisquoc to preserve and protect the archival materials and material culture housed at the museum. Through Sisquoc, Clifford Trafzer began his association with Sherman in 1991 when he became a professor of History and Native American Studies at the University of California, Riverside. He has directed several Ph. D. students who have researched and published on Sherman's colorful past, including Jean Keller, Matthew Sakiestewa Gilbert, Robert McCoy, Kevin Whaler and Leleua Loupe. He has worked with Sisquoc to edit two previous books on Sherman and the American Indian boarding school system. Jeffrey Smith began his association with Sherman in 2002 when he assisted with a national symposium, "Boarding School Blues." Since then, he has extensively researched the photographic collection at the Sherman Indian Museum.

Trafzer, Sisquoc, and Smith began work on this book in 2009 when the authors met at Sherman Indian Museum to discuss the possibility of creating a photographic history of Sherman Institute featuring some of the most striking photographs found in the collection of the school's archives. For many years, we had worked independently on various aspects of Native American history and American Indian education. We had worked together in 2001 and 2002 to sponsor "Boarding School Blues," which we hosted in the auditorium of Sherman Indian High School so current students at Sherman Indian High School could participate. In the past, Sisquoc had worked with two interns of Public History from the University of California, Riverside, to organize portions of the photographic collection at Sherman Indian Museum, but she believed that the dramatic photographic record of Sherman Institute needed to be shared with the larger world. Sisquoc had explained that people respond greatly to historic images, and she believed that a photographic history would capture the attention and inform far more people than the written word. Sisquoc has wanted the world to know more about the rich history of Sherman and its place in American history. She shared this seed of an idea with Jeffrey Smith and Clifford Trafzer, and we agreed to work collectively to create the present work.

Sisquoc led the authors to seek a publisher of high quality and vision. The authors have enjoyed working with an American Indian academic press interested in furthering the voices and images of Native Americans. The authors are deeply grateful that the Pechanga Tribe of Southern California has initiated academic publishing through the Great Oak Press and that the press was interested in our illustrated history of Sherman Institute. Great Oak Press has a vision of publishing academic works on Native Americans of the region and providing voice for indigenous peoples whose stories have been silenced by most university presses that privilege works that silence American Indian people and community-based research that includes voices provided by Native Americans. The authors sincerely thank Great Oak Press and the external reviewers of the press for enhancing this presentation. In particular, the authors extend our appreciation to Thomas Maxwell-Long who guided the publication of this book. We also thank Gary DuBois, Mark Macarro, Andrew Masiel, Sr., Russell Murphy, and the Business Council of the Pechanga Tribe of Luiseño Indians for finding merit in our work and supporting this publication.

We offer this book of selected photographs as historical documents recording some selective aspects of Sherman's history. We have chosen photographs that we considered the most important and appropriate to depict specific topics associated with Sherman's colorful past. Every book is a collaborative effort, and the people of Pechanga and Sherman Institute were instrumental in creating *Shadows of Sherman Institute: A Photographic History of the Indian School on Magnolia Avenue.* During the course of research for this book, the authors examined hundreds of photographs. All of the photographs we selected reside in the archives of Sherman Indian Museum and are published in this volume with the permission of the same museum. Our methodology included working in small groups to collect and interpret photographs. The authors sorted and considered each photograph, organizing them topically. Early on in the research, the authors organized the photographs by topics, not by the era they represented. We decided to highlight the following topics, which have become chapters in this book: Student Life, Student Education, Sports, Music and Fine Arts, Religion and Health, Navajo Program, and Architecture and Built Environment.

After organizing photographs topically, we examined each of them to determine which best depicted the topic we wished to represent. Once we had decided on the photographs for each topic, we scanned them electronically and arranged them in a manner that flowed throughout the chapter. After the initial arrangement, Smith and Trafzer met at the University of Hawai'i, Hilo, to place the photographs in order of presentation. Trafzer worked independently to write and edit the captions to ensure the captions provided authentic, accurate, and useful information. Trafzer also wrote the general introduction and the introductions to each chapter. After submission to the press, the editor of Great Oak Press sent the manuscript to external reviewers. We have reworked the manuscript and taken the constructive recommendations of the reviewers. The authors wish to thank the reviewers for their time and consideration. Their suggestions have enhanced this work.

The authors wish to offer a special thanks to Thomas Maxwell-Long for his interest in the Sherman photographic project and for guiding the manuscript through the various levels of review. We thank Sherman Indian High School and Sherman Indian Museum for hosting our research project, and we thank Leleua Loupe and Jean Keller for their work on the photographic collections at Sherman Indian Museum. Many authors have researched and published on the American Indian boarding school experience, and our work has used many of these past publications. We especially wish to thank the following authors who have researched and published on Sherman Institute, including Jean Keller, Robert McCoy, William O. Medina, Diana Meyers Bahr, Matthew Sakiestewa Gilbert, Kevin Whalen, and Leleua Loupe. We acknowledge the knowledge shared with us by Galen Townsend, Tonita Largo, Daniel Stahl-Kovel, Blossom Hathaway, Robert Przeklasa, Andrew Shaler, Amanda Wixon, Robert Levi, Monica Archuleta, and Hattie Lomayesva. Some of these Native scholars helped us interpret the photographs, and we sincerely appreciate and acknowledge the time and knowledge they shared. We thank the contemporary teachers, counselors, and students at Sherman Indian High School for their gracious and kind support when we have been on campus.

Each author extends a personal thank you to friends and family. Clifford Trafzer wishes to thank Lee Ann, Tess Nashone, Hayley Kachine, Tara Tsaile, Louise Smith, Donna, Sally, Ron, and Al. He thanks his colleagues at the university of California, Riverside, especially Kim Wilcox, Paul D'Anieri, Milagros Peña, Randolph Head, Josh Gonzales, Michelle Raheja, Robert Przeklasa, Rebecca Kugel, and Juliet McMullan. Trafzer also thanks Steven Mandeville-Gamble, Director of Libraries, and his staff for their continual assistance. Lorene Sisquoc wishes to thank her family, especially her children and grandchildren. She also offers her appreciation to Billy Sosa Warsoldier and the volunteers at Sherman Indian Museum. Jeffrey Allen Smith wishes to thank Dani, Allison, April, and Aubrey. He thanks his parents as well as his colleagues at the University of Hawai'i, Hilo, including Michael Bitter, Kerri Inglis, Douglas Mikkelson, Yucheng Qin, and B. Christopher Frueh.

The authors have been privileged to work with the people at Sherman Indian Museum and to have had access to the rich sources housed there. The volunteers, students, staff, and faculty at Sherman have been open and helpful to us and extremely welcoming for many years. We feel honored to have worked on this project with Great Oak Press of the Pechanga Tribe, and we offer our sincere appreciation to the press, editor, and Sherman family.

Clifford E. Trafzer
Jeffrey Allen Smith
Lorene Sisquoc

Riverside, California
December 25, 2015

Introduction

By Clifford E. Trafzer

Sherman Institute casts a long shadow over many years and many people. The Indian school on Magnolia Avenue casts a shadow across the length of Indian Country from the Atlantic to the Pacific and the Great Lakes to Mexico. Like people standing with their back to the sun, their shadow becomes longer and longer as the day progresses and the sun drops into the western sky. Sherman's shadow has become as long as a day, many days through many seasons. This volume presents a few of thousands of images preserved today at Sherman Indian Museum, located on the campus of Sherman Indian High School in Riverside, California, situated halfway between Los Angeles and Palm Springs.[1] The photographs presented here contain shadows of many hues, giving meaning to the school beyond what the viewer sees in each image. Subjects found in each photograph tell a story beyond the visual seen by readers. Each student has a story to share beyond the image we see in photographs. Their collective stories provided the history of Sherman Institute, but no one volume can capture the complete story of the Indian School on Magnolia Avenue.

For this reason, we can only share elements of Sherman's past, a past filled with sorrow and joy and a mixture in-between. In any case, Sherman Institute casts a very long shadow on its students, teachers, superintendents, and staff. It casts the greatest shadow over the Native Nations of the United States that experienced the harvest of forced assimilation, incarceration, and genocide. Children suffered. Adults suffered. Students, tribes, and communities suffered a loss that cannot be overstated. The people lost languages, leadership, parenting skills, health, and future. Yet, in spite of their boarding school seasons, the people survived and took from their boarding school days skills that helped sustain the people and direct them to a better tomorrow. Many Indian students used knowledge and language gained at boarding school to improve and benefit their people. In many ways 'Sherman

I.1 In 1927, music and drama teacher, Mr. Charles Cell, created an impressive touring group of talented students, including (from right to left) Martin Napa, Albert LaRose, Melvin Sidwell, Peter Masten, William Lorentino (Religious Director). Seated in the front is Charles W. Cell. According to the Sherman Bulletin, September 16, 1927, on that day, members of the traveling troupe returned from an automobile tour of the Northwest and Southwest, "staging programs in many of the large cities." They popularized Sherman Institute and raised money for the Protestant Church. According to the school newspaper, the group brought much acclaim to the Indian School on Magnolia Avenue.

Institute casts a long shadow over Native American genocide as defined by the United Nations' Convention on Genocide, 1948.

Unseen Shadows

Every photograph in this collection contains seen and unseen information, particularly about the attempted assimilation of Native American children, but also the student's ability to turn the power to use their boarding school education and experiences to preserve and protect their Native American cultures, languages, and spiritual beliefs.

From some of the photographs, a reader may believe that assimilation worked. In these images, students appeared dressed like most Americans of their time, and they are engaged in activities common to non-Native students throughout the country and the world. Yet, underlining each photograph of a student was the unseen component or shadow of a person's being as a Native American. Students held onto this essence in their hearts and minds, protecting their cultural beings that make them truly indigenous. Hidden in the shadows of the photographs, students maintained their cultures, which they carried forward to their children and grandchildren. Viewers may initially see the students engaged in "civilized" activities living in a modern world, working in various trades, mechanized agriculture, and domestic sciences. But within the shadows, many of these students resiliently held onto their American Indian identities, spiritual beliefs, songs, stories, and cultural heritages. Their shadows contain their commitment to remain Indian and to use their new knowledge to protect and sometimes communicate the depths of their treasured cultures to those that would listen.

Sherman Indian Museum contains thousands of photographs, from old glass plates to modern glossy prints. The authors selected a small body of photographs to share with readers that illustrated some of the central themes found at Sherman Institute. These include Student Life, Student Education, Sports, Music and Fine Arts, Religion and Health, Navajo Program, and Built Environment. The subjects presented here representing Sherman Institute are intended to shed light on the many shadows associated with Sherman Institute from roughly 1902 to 1970, a time before the school became an accredited American Indian high school. Sherman changed over time and the educational opportunities of students changed with the time. No single volume captures the educational experiences at off-reservation American Indian boarding schools, but the work of David Adams, *Education for Extinction*, provides the larger scope of the American Indian boarding school experience.

Diana Bahr, Jean Keller, Kevin Whalen, and Matthew Sakiestewa Gilbert, and Lorene Sisquoc offer the most detailed books on Sherman Institute. These and other authors point out that the American Indian boarding schools were trade schools or industrial-agricultural schools. When Sherman Institute opened in 1902, a boy could learn to be a harness maker, wheelwright, wagon maker, cobbler, builder, farmer, rancher, or blacksmith.[2] By the 1950s, a girl might learn to be a seamstress, beautician, or nurse, depending on the availability of courses and curriculum. Sherman was never static. Sherman's curriculum, built environment and educational mission evolved slowly over time away from assimilation. However, the emphasis on assimilation did not change a great deal over time. Even after the Indian New Deal era of the 1930s and 1940s, Sherman administrators remained committed to assimilation. And although the federal government championed a new, progressive Navajo Program from the 1940s to the 1960s, the school remained staunchly committed to modernity by using formal education to "civilize" Indian students with a distinctly Navajo oriented curriculum.[3]

The authors have presented a few select shadows of Sherman Institute to share the larger picture of one off-reservation American Indian boarding school and to offer viewers a glimpse into various aspects of the school's rich history. Sherman Institute was one of the off-reservation American Indian schools in the United States that changed over time, just as one's shadow changes as the Earth rotates on its axis. Sherman is a part of a national history, unknown or shadowy to most Americans or peoples of the world, because the federal government's aim in creating the boarding schools involved cultural genocide or the attempt to destroy completely the cultures, languages, and spiritual beliefs of American Indians by isolating children from their parents and communities at Sherman Institute, so government administrators, teachers, and disciplinarians could reprogram Native American children into the light of American civilization and culture.

The educational experience at Sherman included a strong element of forced Christianity through an educational structure that forced children to attend church and participate in organizations that emphasized Christianity, including the Young Men's Christian Association (YMCA), Young Women's Christian Association (YWCA), Girl Scouts, and Boy Scouts. These are components of indigenous history during the twentieth century that still influence the course of Native American peoples and their histories today. The school functions today as Sherman Indian High School. It remains an off-reservation American Indian boarding school and living symbol of forced assimilation, incarceration of children, and attempted genocide of Native Americans. Sherman changed over time, and students and officials documented this historical change through the written word and photographic shadows. The present work brings to light a few aspects of Sherman's shadows that offer stories, evidence, and interpretations of a living past.

Contemporary and Past Place of Sherman

Most contemporary students choose to attend Sherman, and they enjoy furthering their educations by attending high school with other Native Americans at Sherman.[4] In the twenty-first century, students attend Sherman for a variety of reasons, including the opportunity to attend school with and meet other American Indians their age from diverse tribes around the United States. They attend Sherman Indian High School to play sports, learn music, develop new educational skills, and engage the academic curriculum. The high school offers students an opportunity to leave home and be on their own among a host of other Native American students from many parts of the United States. The students learn the cultures, songs, and ways of other American Indian students, and they grow in their appreciation of the indigenous diversity known within the Native Universe. But in the past, Sherman served as one of the federal off-reservation American Indian boarding schools the United States had established to destroy American Indian cultures, languages, customs, ceremonies, music, arts, and religions. In the past, some students chose to attend Sherman but many others were forced into an educational system that non-Native superintendents controlled with near total power on a local level.

Policy makers in the United States intended Sherman Institute to be a site of incarceration and control of Native American children where superintendents, teachers, disciplinarians, and matrons could instill Western values in Native American students and help them journey from "savage" to "civilized" human beings. Although the curriculum at Sherman Institute emphasized education and work opportunities for both boys and girls, females had fewer curricular choices on campus. However, females experienced robust opportunities to work off campus through the school's outing program. All off-reservation boarding schools provided educational opportunities for females to work as domestics and males to become tradesmen, with the intention that students would work and move off the reservation. Thousands of American Indian children from numerous Native Nations—constituting a truly transnational group from many Native Nations—attended boarding schools in the United States and residential schools in Canada. Students from many diverse tribes, geographies, and cultures came together at Sherman Institute to learn new forms of music, sports, agriculture, mechanics, nursing, drama, art, and various industrial arts. Some students chose to attend Sherman, but the government forced other young Indian people to attend school in Riverside. In either case, boys and girls made the best of their situation. Some American Indian students used their educations to benefit their people and themselves, thus "turning the power" of the United States and school officials by using their educational experiences to provide benefits to students, their families, and their tribes. Sherman students helped other Native Americans understand the larger systems of the United States, including a system of government that effectuated cultural genocide through attempted assimilation.

Traditional Indigenous Knowledge

Native American students arriving at federal or mission boarding schools arrived with a wealth of knowledge. Born into indigenous people that prized traditional education, students knew a myriad of topics important in their worlds. Since the beginning of creation and thousands of years before Europeans arrived, Native Americans from South, Central, and North America enjoyed rich traditions of educations. Through the oral tradition, mothers and fathers, grandparents, aunts and uncles, and Native teachers taught indigenous children in many intellectual fields through stories, symbols, field trips, and practical experiences. Native American education provided courses of study in mathematics, science, agriculture, aquaculture, art, law, medicine, dance, politics, diplomacy, architecture, history, literature, religious studies, geography, cartography, business, and many other fields of study.[5]

Every American Indian cultural group, tribe, and community had its own way of providing an education, teaching primarily through the oral tradition but also through rock art, intaglios, geoglyphs, landscapes, stars, weather, animals, and plants. Indian teachers taught children math, medicine, science, geography,

cartography, botany, agriculture, art, weaponry, hunting, cooking, home economics, business, history, literature, government, physical education, chemistry, astronomy, mathematics, and a host of other disciplines. Indigenous education originating from North America differed greatly from that developed in Greece, Rome, Europe, Africa, and the Middle East. Most Native American cultures focused centrally on reverence to the earth, animals, plants, and places of indigenous landscapes. Western culture developed strongly from militarism, materialism, writing, banking, architecture, war, and conquest. Although some Native Nations followed suit in some of these areas of cultural development, indigenous cultures of North America differed distinctly. No utopia existed in Native America, but the emphasis of wealth, materialism, banking, and war was far less significant in Native America than in other regions of the world.

Thus, children entering Sherman Institute enjoyed rich and robust systems of education for thousands of years before 1492 when Christopher Columbus spotted the Wakley Islands. However, formal education provided by tribal elders differed remarkably from that children received when they matriculated into Sherman Institute and other off-reservation American Indian boarding schools. In their communities, indigenous grandmothers, grandfathers, aunts, uncles, parents, and tribal leaders trained young people in multiple subjects. They taught children many disciplines through direct instruction and by example. They educated children their songs, stories, art, religion, and environmental sciences. Tribal elders taught children their theory and practical experiences. At Sherman Institute, students learned from teachers in the classroom in the English language and rote learning, which differed greatly from indigenous education. In fact, the entire experience at the Indian boarding schools proved quite different from education on reservations. Formal education at the schools proved frightening and life changing for many Native American students, if not most students entering Sherman. Even before the federal government bought property in Riverside, California, for a new off-reservation American Indian boarding school, educational institutions for Native Americans in the Western Hemisphere had well-defined shadows dating back to the colonial era.

Colonial Education and Native Americans

The Spanish, French, and English established the first American Indian boarding schools at Christian missions designed to convert American Indian children to the religion, culture, and language of European nations. Catholic and Protestant missionaries led the first efforts to "civilize" and Christianize indigenous children of North and South America. Sometimes, Native American leaders wanted their children educated in mission schools so tribal members might better understand the newcomers. In Early America, in areas that became part of the United States, Christian missionaries taught American Indian children about Jesus Christ, the Bible, and European languages. French Catholic priests educated Native American children in Canada, while Protestant ministers spread the gospel among the indigenous people of the Northeast, Middle Colonies, and South.[6] Colonial governments and their educational institutions invited some American Indian students into their covenants to learn Western ways and take their education back to tribal people so they could benefit from the arts of Euro-American "civilization."

In California and the greater American Southwest, Spanish Catholic priests established a series of missions to convert Native Americans to Christianity and educate young people. In the early eighteenth century, Spanish missionaries invaded present-day New Mexico and Arizona, creating missions on the river systems of the Southwest, including the Río Grande and Río Santa Cruz. Missionaries invaded Indian country and took Indian lands where they developed Catholic mission systems among the tribes. In 1769, Father Junípero Serra invaded Alta California, leading the Sacred Expedition. As President of the Sacred Expedition, Serra led his group of settlers northward out of Baja California into Alta California. Serra established Mission San Diego de Acala, the first of twenty-one missions to be situated in Upper California. He located his first mission in present-day San Diego and set out to establish others without the purchase of property or permission of the many tribes that lost resources, land, and lives to the invading parties of priests, soldiers, and civilians.[7]

In spite of the benign version of church history provided by Catholic officials and some scholars, Serra and other missionaries forced themselves on many Indian people, not all, but required neophytes to remain in the mission. Indians had to live by the mission bells, much like school bells, ringing for the neophytes to rise, attend mass, say prayers, go to work, eat meals, pray, and retire. Missionaries taught the Hail Mary and Christian hymns, some of which California Indians incorporated into their own ceremonies, which some use today. Missionaries created a dull and monotonous routine for Native Americans who were born into creative, industrious, and autonomous groups that had survived without European or Christian influences for thousands of years. For generations, the indigenous peoples of California and the Southwest had enjoyed their own autonomy, freedoms, religions, languages, knowledge, and ways of life. They lived daily lives filled with activities, traveling on seasonal rounds, and using well-worn trade routes overland and by sea. They inhabited lands given to them by their Creators and followed laws and codes of morality given to them by their gods—known to them through song and story. Every Indian child learned through the oral traditions of their people and by practical experiences taught to them by father and mothers, uncles and aunts, friends and relatives. The education suited them well for thousands of years without the intervention of newcomers. No utopia existed in California or anywhere else in the Native Universe, but California Indians had a well-ordered life that worked for them, and most of all, they had freedom of choice. Father Serra and other priests actively sought to limit Native American freedoms, especially freedom of religion, speech, assembly, and the right to bear arms.

Life in the missions differed dramatically from traditional Indian life. The priests prevented indigenous freedoms and cultures, attempting to force California Indians into a monotonous mold created by Church fathers. Spanish priests and soldiers forced many California Indians, particularly those living close to the Pacific Coast and near inland areas, into the mission system. Although the Spanish government had legally outlawed slavery, California Indians became a captive labor force, working for free for the good of the missions, not their families

or communities. Father Serra and the priests under him believed it was in the best interest of Native Californians to be forced into the missions and confined in the institutions where priests, soldiers, and Indian overseers forced Indian people to work in the fields, livestock ranges, and church buildings.

Indians worked within the missions without pay, just as Indian students toiled at Sherman Institute and other federal Indian boarding schools worked at the schools for free. When Indians ran away from the mission to live as independent and free people, Catholic priests asked Spanish soldiers from nearby presidios to hunt down wayward neophytes and force them back to the missions. Once soldiers apprehended runaway Indians, Serra permitted severe punishment of runaways, just as boarding school superintendents punished runaway Native American children. Both Spanish and French missionaries employed forced incarcerations, punishments, and food deprivation. Spanish missionaries, with the permission of Father Serra, used whips, shackles, jails, and other punishments. Although Serra did not wield the whips or shackle Indians, he sanctioned corporal punishments, contrary to the teachings of Jesus and St. Francis. Whipping posts at the missions served as powerful reminders to Indians contemplating escape and freedom. Although priests in California and the Southwest, after the 1760s, originated from the Franciscan Order, the priests did not follow the basic teachings of Jesus or the founder of the order, Saint Francis of Assisi.

Neither Jesus nor Saint Francis incarcerated people or had them whipped for transgressions. Serra and other priests sidestepped the teachings of their founders and lessons of peaceful coexistence found in the New Testament. California Indians suffered from corporal punishments. Unfortunately, Santa Barbara Mission Library and Franciscans, Santa Barbara Province Archives in Santa Barbara, California, have silenced scholars interested in researching punishment at the mission. Church archivists have restricted the use of the punishment books that recorded whippings and other punishments sanctioned by the Church meted out to indigenous men, women, and children. Church authorities have likely prohibited the use of the punishment records to suppress documentary evidence

that would show that Father Serra was not a saint.[8] The Church, well known for suppressing unsavory evidence, continues to participate in silencing the historical record that might derail the canonization of Father Serra. Details of these records would prove revealing to the public, which knows little about the violent, oppressive, and deadly system imposed on California's first peoples by missionaries of the Catholic church.

Captain Richard Henry Pratt

In 1878, Congress passed legislation creating the first off-reservation American Indian boarding school, commonly known as Carlisle. The school was the brainchild of veteran Army officer Captain Henry Richard Pratt. The federal government changed its policies toward Native Americans at the close of the American Civil War. During the late nineteenth century, President Ulysses S. Grant and his administration created a new Indian policy that became known as the "Peace Policy." Instead of a government policy of war, death, and destruction of Indian people, the United States set out to corral Native Americans onto Indian reservations where Christian Indian agents, often Protestant ministers, controlled many aspects of Indian social, cultural, spiritual, and economic lives. Reservations became a civilizing instrument of the federal government, a Purgatory where Christians attempted to uplift their Native brothers and sisters. But the reservation system proved to be only one element of the government's new policy. Armed conflict broke out during the era of the Peace Policy, including a war between the United States Army and the combined efforts of such indigenous people of the Southern Plains, including Comanche, Kiowa, Cheyenne, and Arapaho. Like all the Indian wars, the efforts of warriors wore down with time, and the Army ultimately prevailed.

In 1875, during the aftermath of the Red River Wars, the United States Army established prisons for American Indian combatants in Florida, Alabama, Oklahoma, and other sites. The government incarcerated Native American men to punish them for acting as patriots and protecting their families, friends, lands, and tribal rights. Soldiers sent Cheyenne and Kiowa warriors to Fort Marion Prison in St. Augustine, Florida, where Richard Pratt served as superintendent of the prison. During his tenure as prison superintendent, Pratt decided to make his Native charges "useful" by putting them to work. After supervising the Indian prisons, Pratt developed a belief that the Indians had innate intelligence and could learn various trades such as blacksmithing, carpentry, masonry, painting, and other skills. Pratt put Native American prisoners to work at Fort Marion and offered them this form of "formal education." While still at Fort Marion, Pratt determined that he could teach Indians to become part of the citizenry of the United States. He believed Native Americans could be trained in the English language and the social, cultural, and Christian religious culture of the United States.[9]

Captain Pratt believed the key to educating Native Americans was to control their environment through a school system that taught indigenous people vocational instruction. He reasoned that he needed to isolate and control young Indian children and break their connection to traditional culture, language, kinships, arts, and ceremonies. He especially hoped to end the use of ancient American Indian ceremony, ritual, and cultural laws that defined the lives of Native Americans. To effectuate this change, Pratt asked Samuel Armstrong, the Christian superintendent of Hampton Institute to allow Native American students to attend the Institute and join the African American students at the boarding school. As a result, Armstrong allowed a few Native American students to join African American pupils at the school located near Yorktown, Virginia.

Pratt wanted Native American students at Hampton Institute to learn some of the basics of the Three Rs (reading, writing, and arithmetic) and a meaningful trade so they could become "useful" members of American society. Almost from the outset, Pratt clashed with Armstrong. Pratt was a hard driving military man, and while Armstrong had attained the rank of general in the Union Army in his position as superintendent of Hampton Institute, he saw himself as a missionary and philosopher. Pratt's ideas about Indian education and formal leadership conflicted with those of Armstrong, a Christian missionary. Armstrong came from a unique and dedicated Haole family of Christian missionaries from Hawai'i

that Christianized Native Hawai'ians. Born in Maui, Hawai'i, Armstrong was raised by zealot parents that had managed a Christian boarding school for Hawai'ian children. King Kauikeaouli (King Mamehameha III) appointed Armstrong's father the Minister of Public Instruction for the Hawai'ian Kingdom. Young Armstrong established the Hampton Institute to "uplift" the children of former African American slaves. Armstrong and Pratt did not agree on many things, including operation of Hampton Institute. As a result, Pratt asked Congress to support his concept of civilizing American Indians at a school designed solely for Native American students. In 1879, Congress provided Pratt sufficient funding and a workable site at a military base in Carlisle, Pennsylvania, to establish the Carlisle Indian Industrial School.[10]

Carlisle Indian Industrial School

Carlisle Institute emerged as the first off-reservation American Indian boarding school in the United States. Pratt's program of assimilation and genocide became the imprint found at all future Indian boarding schools in the later nineteenth and early twentieth centuries. Sherman would ultimately follow the methodologies employed by Pratt at Carlisle. The first off-reservation American Indian boarding school greatly influenced the development of all Indian schools and its career employees. Through his writings, Pratt laid out his educational philosophy in relationship to Native American children. "It is a great mistake," Pratt proclaimed, "to think that the Indian is born an inevitable savage. He is born a blank, like the rest of us. Left in the surroundings of savagery, he grows to possess a savage language, superstition, and life." Pratt followed in the footsteps of George Washington and Thomas Jefferson, both of whom believed in environmental determinism. Native Americans owed their "savage" ways to their savage environments. As a result, Pratt proposed to remove Native American children from their savage environments to civilize impressionable youngsters to destroy their "uncivilized civilizations," "primitive superstitions," and "savage languages."[11]

According to Pratt, "We make our

greatest mistake in feeding our civilization to the Indians instead of feeding the Indians to our civilization." The Captain felt the federal government must follow an education policy that forced Indians to "swim" in American civilization and Christianity. "The boy learns to swim by going into the water; the Indian will become civilized by mixing with civilization."[12] Pratt's concepts of assimilation became the standard at all the federal Indian boarding schools, including Sherman Institute. As the first superintendent of the Carlisle Indian Industrial School, Pratt approached his job with great enthusiasm and ability to organize resources to make the school a reality. Carlisle became a site of American Indian genocide and transformation by destroying Indian cultures and replacing them with mainstream American civilization.

Pratt faced the building and execution of Carlisle with a missionary zeal. Once he received funding and the old fort in Pennsylvania, the former Army captain began recruiting children as his first students. Among them included some leading Lakota families. During his visit to the Dakotas, Pratt met with Indian leaders and convinced them to send their children to Carlisle. Ota Kte or Plenty Kill, the son of a Lakota chief, was among some of the first children to attend Carlisle. Once at Carlisle, Pratt ordered all the children to change their Native names to English names. Name changes became one of the markers of genocide of American Indians students from "savage" to "civilized". No longer would school officials call Ota Kte by his Native name, but the young lad pointed to the name on a blackboard, which read Luther. As a result, Ota Kte became Luther Standing Bear.[13]

Like other Native American students, Ota Kte lost his name in the boarding school but not his identity. On Indian reservations and at Indian schools, superintendents and teachers changed the names of Native Americans. Tribal censuses and school rolls reveal the fact that non-Indians often changed the names of Native American children, often giving them surnames like Lincoln, Jim, John, Smith, Jones, Jake, and Mike. Years after his boarding school days, Luther Standing Bear used the English language to turn the power and provide a Native American voice to American literature. He wrote several books and articles to tell his story and that of his people. In his book, *My*

People, the Sioux, the American Indian author opened his heart to tell of that day when his father instructed Ota Kte to attend Carlisle and learn as much as he could about the newcomers.[14]

As a youngster, Ota Kte's father, George Standing Bear, had told his son heroic stories of young men dying in battle for the benefit of the people. That was the standard of Native American heroes as found in their rich oral literature. Young warriors preferred to die in battle than die "old and sick." Native American people honor heroes that lived for the good of their communities and families, not their own egos or fortunes. Thus, when his father asked him to go to Carlisle, "I was thinking of my father," Standing Bear wrote, "it occurred to me that this chance to go east would prove that I was brave." Even if the young student died while attending Carlisle, he would die as a hero on a journey to help his people better navigate their relationship with white America. Luther Standing Bear used his schooling to better himself and his people, standing strong against forced use of the English language, strict school rules, severe punishments, and a lonely childhood far from his family, friends, and the culture of Oglala Sioux people.[15]

George Standing Bear wanted his son to attend Carlisle to learn more about newcomers and their way of life. Other parents, especially leaders like George, sent their children to boarding schools for the same reason. Some Native American leaders still sent their children to schools, like Sherman Institute, to advance American Indian sovereignty, self-determination, economic development, and tribal political power. In the past, some parents and relatives of children sent starving children to school so they could eat. Once the United States, state and local governments, and settlers destroyed American Indian economies by taking Indian lands, damming the flow of water sources, fencing hunting and gathering areas, destroying Native habitats, and confining Indians to reservations, Native American populations suffered starvation, malnutrition, diseases, and deaths. To save their children, Indian parents, grandparents, and relatives sent their children to boarding school. This was the case of Comanche Rita Coosewoon who attended the Fort Sill Indian School in Oklahoma and Viola Martinez who attended Sherman Institute.[16] Family members sent these girls and many other school age children to boarding schools to receive food, clothing, and shelter so they could live. Several families did the same thing, sending their children off to school as a means of survival. Other times, children chose to go to boarding school where they could play sports, learn new musical instruments, meet other Indians, or learn a trade.

Perris Indian School

Sherman Institute developed out of a school system conceived and executed by Superintendent Pratt of the Carlisle Indian Industrial School. After thirteen years of training American Indian students, Carlisle had created a lengthy shadow that extended to Southern California. By the last decades of the nineteenth century, several students from Southern California tribes had attended Carlisle or one of the other off-reservation boarding schools. Native Americans in Southern California and officials working within the Mission Indian Agency pressured the Office of Indian Education to create an Indian school in the region. In 1892, the lobbying for an Indian school in Southern California bore fruit with the establishment of a federal Indian boarding in the rural community of Perris, California, located a few miles south of Riverside.

Superintendents and teachers at the Perris Indian Industrial School offered classes in basic reading, writing, and arithmetic as well as industrial arts, domestic sciences (home economics), and agriculture. Children from many reservations around the United States attended the Perris School, but the heaviest concentration of indigenous students at Perris called Southern California their home. Over the decade from 1892 to 1902, several students at Perris hailed from the Pechanga, La Jolla, Cahuilla, Soboba, Campo, and other reservations located in Southern California. In the late 1890s, Harwood Hall became the school superintendent at Perris. He was a career employee of the United States Indian Service, having served at the Phoenix Indian School before leading the Perris Indian School. Like several school superintendents, Hall also served as an Indian agent, although he and his wife preferred working with school age children at federal schools for Native Americans.

While assigned to Perris Indian School, located in a rural ranching and farming area south of Riverside, Hall grew to dislike the isolated setting far from an urban area and its associated amenities. He sought a reason to remove the school to a city in Southern California and used the excuse of poor and inadequate water supply to convince the Office of Indian Education to move Perris Indian School to Riverside, a prosperous young city founded a few decades before. Riverside had emerged as a wealthy frontier city with extensive citrus farms. From the time Hall arrived at the Perris School, he began campaigning to establish a new boarding school to be located in Riverside, a budding urban area and citrus agricultural center of inland Southern California. With the help of Riverside business and political interests, in 1901, the Office of Indian Affairs agreed to build a new off-reservation American Indian boarding school.[17]

Harwood Hall and Frank Miller

Harwood Hall found a significant ally in Frank Miller, a powerful Riverside businessman, entrepreneur, and owner of the Glenwood Mission Inn, today the famous hotel on Mission Avenue in downtown Riverside. As historian Nathan Gonzales has pointed out, "without Frank Miller, Sherman would never have been relocated into Riverside." Contemporary scholar and Miwuk Indian William Medina has pointed out that Frank Miller wanted Indians at the Mission Inn Hotel as part of the illusion that his hotel, built in 1901-1902 in the Mission Revival architectural style, had once served as one of the Spanish missions. Miller was so invested in the establishment of Sherman Institute that he built a trolley running on Magnolia Avenue from the Mission Inn to Sherman Institute that carried passengers to tour the school. Next door to Sherman, Miller built Riverside's first zoo. Visitors to the Mission Inn could purchase a package excursion to see the Indians at Sherman and walk next door to the zoo and Miller's monkeys and other animals confined in cages. Like the students next door, the animals at Chemawa Park were incarcerated by force into an unnatural environment and institution created by individuals that believed it was in the best interest of the animals for their own preservation—not unlike the Native American students next door at Sherman Institution.[18]

Government officials, business interests, and the general public of Riverside welcomed the establishment of Sherman Institute. The Indian school on Magnolia Avenue brought a new and cheap labor force to work at the citrus groves, local farms, ranches, packing houses and hotels, especially the Mission Inn, the faux Spanish mission that employed Sherman students to promote the ruse of historical authenticity of an Indian mission. The school brought long-term contracts of federal money into the region and offered a tourist attraction where visitors could visit "real Indians," take pictures of Indian children and magnificent buildings, in the Mission Revival style, and enjoy the company of Native American students who acted as tour guides. The school hired local Indian and non-Indian employees. Visitors to the Indian school, including American Indian parents, spent money when visiting the school. In addition, the Sherman sports teams, bands, choral groups, and thespians brought in money to Riverside and the school. Children presented new cultural elements to the region and generated additional dollars. Sherman became a boon to the local economy, and it proved a positive factor for the development of the growing business interests of the inland area of Southern California.

Cornerstone and Time Capsule at Sherman Institute

On July 18, 1901, several non-Native men and women gathered near the corner of Jackson and Magnolia avenues in Riverside, California, to lay the cornerstone of the newest off-reservation American Indian boarding school. They had named the school Sherman Institute after the Honorable James Schoolcraft Sherman, Chairman of the Committee on Indian Affairs in the House of Representatives— not Civil War General William Tecumseh Sherman. James Schoolcraft Sherman was a conservative but affable Republican member of the United States House of Representatives from New York for 20 years. He was Chair of the Indian Affairs Committee. In 1900, he convinced Congress to approve an appropriation of $75,000 to build a new Indian school in Riverside, California. In acknowledgment of his efforts, the Indian Office named Sherman Institute in his honor. Later, from 1909-1912, Sherman served as Vice-President to President William Howard Taft.

Sherman Institute became the twenty-fifth off-reservation American Indian boarding school, patterned after Captain Pratt's model of an industrial school. In fact, Richard Pratt sent a congratulatory telegram to Sherman, which the founders placed in a large copper time capsule that also included a letter from President William McKinley, Rules for the Indian School Service, photographs, and an inspiring speech by California's United States Senator George C. Perkins. In the spirit of assimilation and Christian duty, Perkins proclaimed that the new industrial school would be erected "for the glory of God," the Creator and "our Father and the Father of all races of mankind."[19]

Senator Perkins told the crowd assembled at the Sherman site that God had "taught us the brotherhood of man, and… their responsibility for the care of others." Thus, Sherman Institute would "be erected… for the redemption of a race" and "enable the Indian, who can no longer exist in a wild state, … to meet the requirements of modern progress" and learn to "secure for himself the best there is in our civilization." Perkins and the other Christian reformers around him believed they were acting in the interest and for the betterment of all Native Americans for their own betterment and "the Glory of the great God whom we all revere." Perkin's represented the reformist spirit of white Americans, reformers that believed they had a holy obligation to uplift their "red" neighbors by destroying the backward, primitive, and savage ways of Indians. As a result, like the other boarding schools, Sherman teachers and administrators committed genocide to destroy American Indian languages, beliefs, music, songs, history, foods, clothing, laws, manners, and cultural heritages.[20]

Like other federal Indian off-reservation boarding schools, white reformers believed that Sherman Institute would become an instrument of the federal government to separate Native children from their parents, grandparents, families, and tribes so that non-Indian teachers and administrators could capture, isolate, and reprogram Native American children to speak, write, think, and act like white Americans of the early twentieth century. In this way, the school would serve as a civilizing space where indigenous children could become civilized Christians, useful workers, and a part of the dominant society. Sherman existed to undermine Native American sovereignty, self-determination, religion, art, and language. The Indian school on Magnolia Avenue intended to supplant American Indian culture with that of the so-called civilized American society as defined by newcomers of the United States. In sum, Sherman Institute was a site of genocide and incarceration to control and assimilate Native American children. American reformers had little faith that older Indians would ever change, but they believed by separating children from their Native families and placing them in a controlled built environment, reformers could forever change American Indian children and the future of Native Americans within the American republic.

Perris Indian School to Sherman Institute

Even before Sherman opened its doors for school in September 1902, Superintendent Harwood Hall had most of the children at Perris Indian School transferred to Sherman Institute where children slept in tents and helped build the school through their hard labor. Hall and his wife were zealots of Indian assimilation through education and hard work. Historian David Adams has labeled the process of destroying Indian civilizations and languages through assimilation as "Education for Extinction."[21] This is an apt description of the forced assimilation policies initiated at Carlisle by Pratt and carried out at Sherman by Hall and his successors. As soon as Hall arrived on the Sherman campus in Riverside, he began to shape the curriculum at the new Indian school on Magnolia Avenue. As he had at Phoenix Indian School and Perris Indian School, at Sherman Institute, Hall emphasized vocational and agricultural education, giving only sparing concern to academics. He also established the Outing Program at Sherman, which placed Indian boys and girls into homes, businesses, and farms in Southern California and beyond to labor as a form of education. Initially at Sherman, the Indian girls were in greater demand than boys for the Outing Program. Although details of abuses are not common, girls sometimes demanded that superintendents at Sherman remove them from a home because of conflicting issues, at times related to sexual advances. According to historian Kevin Whalen, school documents indicate that Sherman girls formed friendships and coalitions while working in Los Angeles and other cities, watching over and helping each other as sisters.[22]

Non-Indian families wanted Sherman girls to live in their homes as babysitters, housecleaners, and domestics. Most often older female students lived in the homes of white citizens, serving as maids and baby sitters. Male students worked and lived on ranches, farms, packinghouses, and iron works. They tended horses, cattle, and other livestock. Both male and female students picked citrus and soft fruit. They also cultivated, planted, tended, weeded, watered, and harvested many varieties of vegetables, especially at Fontana Farms north of Sherman at the base of the San Gabriel Mountains. Girls and boys worked for low wages, which employers sent to Superintendent Hall who controlled the money boys and girls earned. Hall oversaw a school bank and managed student earnings. Although students often earned less than other employees doing the same work, many students appreciated the job and the money they earned. In fact, Whalen has documented many school children, often in their teens, using Sherman's Outing or work program, as an employment agency.[23]

Robert Levi, a Cahuilla Indian from the Torres Martinez Reservation and former Sherman student, once commented, "We were glad to get money and have a job. We didn't have money from home, so with the jobs through outing we had money to buy a soda or candy and we had money to send home to help our parents."[24] Historian Whalen provided an example of one Navajo boy who took a variety of jobs so he could earn sufficient money to buy a flock of fifty sheep. With the money he earned from working through the Outing Program, he could return to the reservation and begin his life as a sheep rancher. In a sense, he could return home to Dinetah a rich young man with an immediate start in his chosen profession. While attending Sherman, students lived like little soldiers. Boys and girls wore military uniforms and learned to march in formation like little cadets. Every morning they participated in a flag ceremony to honor the Stars and Stripes, and they learned to drill. Captain Pratt, the former Army officer, had instituted this tradition at Carlisle, and boys attending Indian boarding schools became so well trained in military life that they found it easy to transition from school into the armed services of the United States. Over the last hundred years, several of Sherman's men and women have served in the military, some giving their lives protecting freedoms often denied Indians before and after 1924 when Indians became citizens of the United States.

In addition to working off campus through the Outing Program, Hall and other superintendents put children to work throughout the Sherman campus and farms doing any number of jobs from sewing sheets and pillowcases to building mangers from which the meat and dairy cattle ate. Before Sherman opened for classes in 1902, Hall transferred most of the children from Perris to Riverside where they worked on the Sherman construction site. At that time, Hall began their practical instruction in domestic science and industrial arts—building the campus. Before the days of child labor laws, Hall had the children mixing mortar, laying bricks, cementing sidewalks, erecting fences, planting trees, seeding grass, painting buildings, stuccoing walls, and helping in many ways to construct the school. Hall was eager to have the school children learn modern industrial trades and domestic sciences so they could, one day, be a part of the market economy with knowledge of the English language and the broader belief system of capitalism, consumerism, and materialism. Child labor at Sherman and beyond was part of the federal design to make Indians "useful."

Popular literature and the press portrayed indigenous men, women, and children as lazy, unmotivated, and communal. This common trope was a total misconception of indigenous peoples of the Americas, as they had always been highly industrious through art, architecture, music, dance, drama, song, farming, fishing, hunting, and gathering. During Hall's era of the late nineteenth and early twentieth centuries, Native Americans had seen the newcomers destroy their indigenous economic life ways. Rather than starve to death after white hunters killed the buffalo or settlers had stolen the water resources and best farmlands, Native Americans had sought day labor in the non-Native market in order to survive. In large part, Native Americans endured the transitional era of Native American history by working for cash money to feed, clothe, and house their families. Most American reformers and policy makers ignored this fact, including Hall who felt it was his obligation to "change" Native Americans and make them industrious through a curriculum that included a heavy dose of hard work at the school and beyond the school grounds.

Harwood Hall and future superintendents of Sherman Institute intended to teach Native American students "new values" of hard work so Indian students could discard their indigenous beliefs in communal living, cooperation, and consensus decision making. Hall and the instructors at Sherman perceived these values as primitive or savage, which they hoped to place with rugged individualism. Romaldo LaChusa, a "Mission Indian" from Southern California became the first American Indian student enrolled at Sherman Institute, and over the years, thousands of Native American children followed in his footsteps.[25] Many California Indians, including those from the Pechanga, Cahuilla, Soboba, Morongo, San Manuel, Rincon, La Jolla, Campo, and other reservations in Southern California attended Sherman Institute. Contemporary tribal citizens among California's First Nations know a great deal about Sherman Institute because their relatives once attended the boarding school.

Reservation superintendents, Christian missionaries, schoolteachers, and indigenous parents sent children to Sherman Institute. When children stepped off the wagons, buses, or trolleys that had brought them up to the Magnolia Avenue entrance to the school, an impressive but intimidating sight met their eyes. In front of them rose an imposing scene of rolling hills, trees and shrubs as well as multistory buildings that posed an impressed site along the southern horizon. The school consisted of massively thick buildings, some of them tall, multiple-storied buildings—likely the tallest buildings many reservation children had ever seen. City officials in Riverside and those of the Office of Indian Affairs built Sherman in a budding new architectural style called Mission Revival. Like the Mission Inn Hotel, architects created Sherman Institute to appear somewhat like the missions and other adobe and rock buildings constructed during the Spanish colonial era of the twenty-one Catholic missions founded in Alta California. Construction crews, American Indian students, and hired workman built Sherman Institute in the Mission Revival style. The new mission style used some aspects of the old mission style but modernized it to suit the aesthetic concept of modern architects and the practical needs of the early twentieth century. The neo-mission revival style resembled the public representations of the Spanish mission system, offering a very romanticized presentation of the Mission era of California's past. For California Indians, Sherman's appearance as a neo-mission may have offered painful memories of stories told by tribal elders about their family's days in the missions. Historians, Western writers, novelists, artists, and architects created their own image of the past era, in part to attract tourists to Southern California. The architecture found at Sherman Institute represented an idealized, sanitized, and mythical past but provided an architectural style that fascinates today.[26]

Even before American Indian children arrived at Sherman Institute, the genocidal process of forced assimilation began. School officials separated boys and girls, taking them into a cold, impersonal space where the children were stripped of their clothing and stood naked waiting for inspection for "defects." Schoolteachers and disciplinarians removed the children of more than their clothing. They attempted to strip them of their identities as American Indians. School officials confiscated their Indian dress, taking away their shirts, skirts, pants, and other articles of Native clothing. They confiscated (and sometimes kept) the dolls, charms, jewelry, purses, pouches, bags, and beadwork they had brought from home. Sometimes, their parents, grandparents, aunties, and uncles had made these items for the children. Taking these items was a part of the assimilation process, intended to tear the relationship of the children from their people.

When children entered Sherman, they lost their personal items that had originated out of their communities. Students at Sherman often arrived with many material items made by friends and family members. Students lost their Native clothing, purses, bags, hair ornaments, medicine bundles, toys, and moccasins. Some of the items the staff took from them included sacred objects. A barber cut the hair of both girls and boys, often cutting or shaving their hair, a point of pride among many Native Americans, short or shaving it completely off. Assistants to the school superintendent forced each child to shower, an event totally new to nearly all the students during the early twentieth century, as most reservation homes had little running water or few indoor bathrooms. After the scrub down, a nurse or doctor inspected each child for "defects." Medical assistants looked for lice, bleeding gums, trachoma, tuberculosis, pneumonia, rickets, scabies, ring worm, broken bones, rotten teeth, oozing sores, or other ailments. Once Western healthcare providers had completed this procedure, school aids issued each child a new set of clothes, a uniform resembling a military outfit.

Boys and girls looked like young Army cadets, and photographs make them look very similar to one another during the first decades of the school's history. The military introduction of Native American students to Sherman Institute removed all tangible vestiges of American Indian culture, the children were outwardly rendered homogeneous. Induction into Sherman offered another phase of the assimilation process administered by the Office of Indian Affairs through the school. However, inspection of Indian students for "defects" also led to the discovery of tuberculosis among the students and provided an opportunity for school officials to contact agents to encourage them to have the family of students examined for the dreaded disease. At Sherman, officials made a point of teaching students basic elements of public health, including information about how to detect tuberculosis within their bodies and those of others. To reinforce public health knowledge, the school newspaper, *The Sherman Bulletin*, May 15, 1918 published this poem about tuberculosis:

I will wash my hands before each meal today.

I will drink a glass of water before each meal and before going to bed.

I will brush my teeth in the morning and in the evening today.

I will take ten or more slow deep breaths of fresh air today.

I will play outdoors or with windows open more than thirty minutes today.

I will be in bed ten hours or more each night and keep my windows open.

I will try to sit up and stand up straight, to eat slowly, and to attend to toilet and each need of my body at its regular time.

I will take a full bath on each day of the week.

Based on the model established by Captain Richard Pratt, Sherman Superintendent Harwood Hall and future school heads had the students marching to and from events, emulating students at military boarding schools of the era. Hall created a regulated and very predictable life for students at Sherman Institute. Like many boarding schools, Sherman used bells to provide an ordered life. Bells rang to wake the children. Bells rang to tell them when to eat in the school cafeteria. Bells rang to signify the start and end of classes. Like the bells used at the Spanish missions, bells punctuated every aspect of student life from morning to bedtime. Life at Sherman Institute proved very regulated for Native school children. Rather than treat the children as children, school officials treated boys differently than girls. But administrators and teachers treated all children like "little" adults, drilling them as if they were miniature soldiers and preventing them from growing up with the love and warmth of their families and friends back on the reservations.

Students of all ages, from five to twenty-five, attended Sherman Institute. They could not eat or leave the table in the cafeteria without permission. Boys and girls had to salute the superintendent, respect the Stars and Stripes, and march in formations. Every Sunday, school officials forced children to attend a Catholic or Protestant church service, preferably at one of the churches located immediately off campus. The federal government had created Sherman as a secular institution, but Sherman never separated church and state. In 1902, American Indians were not citizens of the United States and had no rights as citizens of any state or the country.

At Sherman and the other boarding schools, officials forced children to attend Christian churches or face punishment. On Saturday, Catholic children also attended catechism, a common educational event for nearly all Catholic children. Often they chose to attend the church that offered the best food or finest prizes for learning Bible verses. Many students learned to navigate this system of assimilation to the delight of school and church officials, while at the same time, holding onto their traditional religious beliefs. School superintendents also expected Native American students to participate in the Boy Scouts, Girl Scouts, Young Men's Christian Association (YMCA), and the Young Women's Christian Association (YWCA). These organizations played a role on the Sherman campus as organizations supportive of assimilation, patriotism, and Christian ideals. [27]

Students lived in dormitories where men or women watched over them and punished them for infractions. Children lived without the guidance of their parents and grandparents, aunts and uncles. Boarding school children had no parenting role models, and they did not develop parenting skills. The lack of parenting skills has long plagued Native American communities of North America, and American Indian leaders today recognize the consequences of federal officials breaking up families through the forced removal of school children to boarding schools . Some school employees proved to be loving and caring, but others could be cold and cruel, whipping and jailing children. Child and sexual abuse occurred at times at the schools, and former boarding school children have had to live a life of humiliation and shame stemming from forced sexual abuse perpetrated against boys and girls alike. Past sexual abuse at off-reservation American Indian boarding schools continue to plague some students. Sexual abuse has created social and familial problems within some Native American communities today. Some indigenous people believe that superintendents, teachers, and staff members failed to protect children from perpetrators of abuse, and adults who attended the schools continue to suffer trauma as a result of their experiences.[28]

Superintendents had great control over the lives of American Indian students at Sherman Institute and the other boarding schools. Superintendents could (and did)

prevent children from leaving campus to visit their home, and they could block parents from seeing their children, even after parents had traveled many miles to Sherman to see their children. Sometimes school children remained separated from their families for eight to twelve years, depending on the wishes of superintendents. At Sherman Institute, children had little recourse but to obey superintendents, since the school held students captive. Some children spent their entire childhood at Sherman Institute or at one of the other boarding schools. Students spent most of their time learning a vocational trade and fundamental academics.

Outing Program and Runaways

During their days at Sherman Institute, many children participated in the Outing Program, which took students off campus to work away from the school. Non-Indians often employed Indian girls to babysit, cook, and clean. Farmers and ranchers employed Sherman boys to feed, herd, kill, and butcher livestock or cultivated crops. Sherman students worked in many vocations, some of which led them to employment beyond Sherman in towns and cities across the United States. Some Sherman students learned trades that proved worthless on the reservations, such as cooking for three thousand people three times a day in a modern kitchen or washing, drying, and mending clothing for several thousand people. Reservations had little capacity to support cobblers, chefs, barbers, welders, carpenters, wheelwrights, masons, mechanics, machine shop workers, or operators of modern farming equipment. As a result, when students returned to their homes, they found they had mastered trades not applicable to reservation life, which sometimes led to migration of former Sherman students off reservations to seek meaningful employment.

Some students attended Sherman just to learn a trade or work through the Outing Program to earn money. Others came to the school to learn music, play sports, or follow in their parents' footsteps. But the government forced other children into Sherman. Like the Spanish missionaries, officials of the United States forced some children into Sherman Institute

and other federal boarding schools. At Sherman, Indian children occasionally fled the school. One such student included Serrano student Francis Morongo from the San Manuel Indian Reservation in San Bernardino, California. Francis remembered, "We had to wear uniforms, and we marched everywhere we went." She resented having to march and salute superintendents, saying "We had to salute that man whenever we saw him." Francis was taken to Sherman as a young girl and found herself totally disoriented. She did not know where "the white people had taken me." She knew she was at the school but not where the school was located in relationship to her home on the San Manuel Indian Reservation. She was lonely, stressed, and afraid. As a tribal elder in her 80s, she stated that while she was a Sherman student, her physical and mental condition led to an illness and her admittance into the Sherman hospital. The nurses directed her to a bed on the second floor of the hospital where she began her recovery.

From her hospital bed, she could look northeast and clearly see the mountains above her home. "I could see my home; I could see the reservation and the foothills and the reservation; this made me feel good to see my home, but I was homesick." From her hospital bed, Francis could see the great Arrowhead cut naturally into the face of the southern slope of the San Bernardino Mountains that overlooks the San Manuel Indian Reservation. Once she saw the Arrowhead, she could orient herself. She also knew what she needed to do—flee Sherman Institute. When she felt better, she made her plan to escape in the dark during the early hours of the morning as everyone slept. This little girl, about in second grade, made her escape from forced incarceration. The youngster fled the Sherman hospital and the school grounds. She navigated her way through the rural part of Riverside north of Sherman, walking day and night through Riverside and Colton. She walked through San Bernardino, finally making it home to Highland, California, and the welcoming arms of her parents on the San Manuel Indian Reservation. She never returned to boarding school but finished her education in the public schools of San Bernardino.[29]

No doubt school officials tried to find Francis Morongo after she ran away from Sherman, but to no avail. Not all child runaways from Sherman were so fortunate. Student attitudes toward Sherman Institute varied widely from student to student. Some students championed the school and others hated it. For example, in 1917, Miwuk students Lillian Franklin and her little brother, Bill Franklin, attended Sherman Institute. Lillian enjoyed her time at Sherman and thrived on the academic experience. She remained at the school content to learn and grow. When she was in her teens, she met Oscar Medina at a picture show. The couple fell in love and eventually married. Their family today includes William, Jon, Max, and Susie, prominent members of Riverside society. While Lillian reveled in her education at Sherman, her brother did not. Bill Franklin so disliked the institution that he ran away, walking over five hundred miles to get home. Franklin, who later became a political and spiritual leader of Miwok people, so disliked Sherman that he walked from Riverside to his village in present-day El Dorado County, a rural area east of Sacramento in the heart of his band of Miwok people.[30]

Language Loss and Cultural Preservation

When Sherman officials realized a child was missing, the non-Native people hunted them down and punished them. If school officials caught truant students, administrators ordered them punished by whipping, solitary confinement, ridicule, food deprivation, and other means. Each school had disciplinarians who meted out corporal punishments for boys and girls. Sherman officials also punished children for speaking their Native languages. Sherman student Viola Martinez, a Paiute Indian from the eastern side of the Sierra Nevada Mountains, entered the Institute with her mind made up: "I was not going to forget my language." As a result, she practiced her language "every chance I got" often running off with her cousins "so we could talk Paiute." She and her cousin, Evelyn, climbed into the palm trees situated around campus "where we wouldn't be seen or heard." But some of the other students found Viola and Evelyn speaking Paiute and informed on them. The head matron punished both girls, forcing them to scrub out "this huge bathroom… showers and bowls and toilet seats." Years later, Viola remembered they

had to clean "every inch" of the bathroom. As a result of conditions imposed on Native American students about speaking their indigenous languages, Viola lost her language that she had treasured as a child. This was a casualty of the boarding school system and forced assimilation. Some Paiute people ostracized Viola for losing her language, but like many children, rules and punishments at boarding schools rendered her loss of language.[31]

Missionary experiences in dealing with Native American children offered one template for federal officials used to "civilize" and Christianize Native American children. Policy makers of the United States drew upon Christian missionary systems as part of its model in the creation of Sherman Institute. As during the Spanish colonial era, some indigenous parents chose to send their children into the mission system. Some Native American parents wanted their children to learn about the Christian faith, and they encouraged school officials to have their children attend church, Sunday school, and organizations sponsored by Christian groups. However, far more parents preferred their children to keep their indigenous faiths, ceremonies, songs, and beliefs. Nevertheless, Sherman and the other schools worked diligently to destroy Native American religions, songs, and ceremonies. Generally, students could not practice their cultural practices at the schools, causing some children to meet in the orange groves adjacent to Sherman where they sang and prayed. When possible, the students met in a communal setting in the orange groves to eat Native foods and learn new songs from classmates. Sometimes these rendezvous led to marriages between Indian students from diverse backgrounds, causing a Native American diaspora and new family relationships between diverse tribal members.

While some students ran away from Sherman, others enjoyed their boarding school days where they played sports, socialized with other Indians, marched in school bands, played in the orchestra, sang in the choir, and made lasting friends. Many couples fell in love at Sherman Institute, and a few photographs show students getting married on campus or at churches immediately off campus. Some married student couples had children while attending Sherman. Over the years, a loyalty toward Sherman developed, and former students sent their children to

school at the boarding school on Magnolia Avenue. Thus, in spite of forced assimilation, harsh punishments, and limited educational options, some students grew attached to the school, which became their own, and many remembered their school days fondly. No question that the federal government established Sherman and the other boarding schools to destroy American Indian cultures, languages, and religions, but something more dynamic happened at Sherman, which has given it a lasting place within the history of Native America. The school changed over the years and offered some children academic and vocational opportunities they would not have had otherwise. Thus, the legacy of Sherman Institute is complex and much like a shadow that changes over time depending on the angle of light and position of the person involved. Each student, superintendent, and structure has its own unique experience and left shadows of former boarding school days.

Choosing to Attend Sherman Institute

Quechan student Lee Emerson, attended Fort Yuma School located in the old buildings of the fort on the California side of the Colorado River adjacent to Yuma, Arizona. After finishing sixth grade in the 1930s, Emerson had a chance to attend Sherman Institute and eagerly agreed to go to Riverside or "The Land of Oranges." He wanted to go to Sherman so he could learn to play musical instruments. Emerson fondly remembered playing sports but his real passion was music. He recalled Sherman as the place where he learned to play the trombone and participate in many musical performances. At Sherman, he played in the marching band, school orchestra, and sang in the Sherman choir. Emerson proved to be a talented singer, and he joined the choir where he excelled singing classical music, jazz, and blues. He also learned Christian songs, which he would later use as the choir director of churches in the Yuma area. He also remembered playing sports, which he loved.[32]

When Emerson returned home to the Fort Yuma Quechan Reservation, he found work as a choir director because of his skills as a musician and singer. Churches near Ft. Yuma Quechan Reservation hired him as their musical director. In addition, Emerson joined the famous Fort Yuma Indian Band, traveling around the United States performing in many venues, including inauguration parades and the Rose Parade in Pasadena, California. To earn extra money for his family, Emerson joined local bands, playing trombone and other instruments at dances, bars, receptions, and other events. At one point of his life, during World War II, Emerson put his Sherman education to work in the shipyards of Los Angeles as a welder. At Sherman, Emerson had learned to be an expert welder, a skill Lee also employed while working for the Bureau of Reclamation. In spite of his education at the Fort Yuma Indian Boarding School and Sherman Institute, Emerson never lost his Native language, culture, religion, or historical knowledge. He became the Quechan tribal historian, the most celebrated and knowledgeable person within the Quechan community about the ancient and recent past of his people. In addition to his life's work, Lee Emerson educated many students of Native American history about the heritage and spiritual beliefs of his people.[33]

Another former Sherman Student, Matthew Hanks Leivas, attended the Institute during the late 1960s and early 1970s. Leivas grew up on the Colorado River Indian Reservation with other Chemehuevi, Mohave, Navajo, and Hopi people. His mother, Gertrude Leivas, had attended and graduated from Sherman, and Matthew grew up hearing stories about Sherman Institute. When Gertrude had attended Sherman, the school's sports teams had gained much success and notoriety throughout Southern California as a sport powerhouse. Leivas was a superior athlete, known throughout the reservations along the Colorado River as a formidable athlete in football, baseball, basketball, track, and wrestling.[34]

During his middle school years, Leivas decided to leave the reservation and seek a larger playing field at Sherman Institute. He attended Sherman Institute to play football where he became the star athlete at the time. The students then attending Sherman Institute in the late 1960s and early 1970s also elected Leivas to serve as Student Body President, a leadership position Leivas took seriously. He worked with the administration, the Bureau of Indian Affairs, and the student body to have the Office of Indian Education change

Sherman from an Institute to Sherman Indian High School. In 1970, the Office of Indian Education agreed to change Sherman to an accredited high school, a distinction the campus has held ever since.

Like Emerson and others, Leivas enjoyed his school days at Sherman, remembering them as one of the highlights of his life. Like other Sherman students, Matthew Leivas turned the negative power of assimilation into a positive life. He kept his indigenous culture and his language. Leivas learned a complex body of Salt Songs, and he has been a part of an inter-tribal effort of Southern Paiute people to preserve and present the ancient Salt Songs. He joined the board of the Native American Land Conservancy, which has been instrumental in preserving the Salt Songs. Leivas has worked for his tribe as a farmer, cultivating the desert using irrigation water from the Colorado River. Leivas is a tribal historian and has contributed to the research studies by several university scholars. Leivas and Emerson are only two of thousands of Native Americans that used their formal educations at Sherman to benefit themselves, their families, and their people. Many students returned to their communities fulfilling the role of traditional heroes found in the oral literature of Native Americans of North America. The Quechan still revere Lee Emerson and honor the example he set for others, and Chemehuevi recognize the cultural contribution of Matthew Hanks Leivas.

Cameras, Images, and Shadows

Since Sherman Institute opened its doors in 1902, the shadows of thousands of Indian students have passed through the school halls, walked the school grounds, and labored on and off campus.[35] The archives of the Sherman Indian Museum as well as the National Archives offer numerous written documents, providing part of the historical record about the school children. The Sherman Indian Museum also contains over ten thousand images that very few people have seen or analyzed. They provide another form of documentation often overlooked as an historical source, and sources that require careful examination, analysis, and interpretation.

The entire photographic collection at

the Sherman Indian Museum includes glass plates, black and white photographs, and recent color images of students. Many of the earlier photographs originated from school officials or representatives of the Office of Indian Education as propaganda and served as verifying the positive benefits of the national assimilation program. School administrators posed many images to illustrate success assimilating young Native American students from "savage" to "civilized" human beings prepared to enter the labor force of the United States as useful servants of the market economy. Cameras clicked away producing black and white images demonstrating that all the Indian students at Sherman Institute loved their educational experiences. Photographs served as visual messages intended for public consumption and for politicians who determined the budget for Sherman Institute and the off-reservation American Indian boarding school system. As a result, some photographs are sanitized and idealized, but they offer one important window into Sherman Institute. Most of the photographs reflect young people in transition and making the best of their time at school. Many images represent the fact that Sherman boys and girls turned the power imposed on them and made the best of their boarding school days. In this way, many children became heroes of survival, using their educations to better themselves and their people.

Photographic compositions of Sherman Institute and its students depict themes and subjects important to the photographer and those paying the photographers. The subjects presented are those photographers and administrators wished the public to see, not necessarily what students would have liked to convey to their parents, people, or public. Viewers of Sherman photographs will see well-groomed, clean students. They wear new styles of clothing that change over time. Viewers witness young children marching as cadets, patriotic pupils, and hard-working children being useful to the school, their families, and the Republic by exhibiting the ideals of rugged individualists. The lens of many cameras capture evidence of Christianity through photographs of Christmas pageants, gift exchanges, colorful, Christmas trees, and church activities. Cameras captured the surface of each student, but viewers are asked to look much deeper to see the shadows behind each student, building, and event.

Native America and Sherman Shadows

All of Sherman's students were Native Americans, born of the various Indian nations of the United States. Within each student dwelled a living culture of unique languages, religions, songs, stories, and beliefs, mostly hidden from the camera lens but casting their human shadow. Images found at Sherman Indian Museum speak of a new circumstance and situation for most students, confined in a socio-economic educational system that did not value traditional Native American cultures, languages, histories, religions, or ways of economic life. The photographs reflect the high value non-Indians placed on new forms of work and industry as well as new gender roles for boys and girls. Many of the photographs feature female children being highly industrious in the domestic sphere, putting them in the same place expected of the dominant society, which devalued the role of professional and educated women. Photographers feature many Native American females at work washing clothes, sewing clothing, and ironing sheets. The photographs feature gender roles well established for girls in the twentieth century who were to fulfill their destinies as housewives, mothers, and maids. However, the image-makers also included some photographs of Sherman women playing sports, mastering musical instruments, riding bicycles, and leading the band as baton twirlers. By and large, however, administrators wanted to portray Sherman females within the domestic sphere, not as equals.

Far more academic and vocational opportunities existed at Sherman for boys than for girls, but these educational opportunities trained boys in the industrial arts, mechanical sciences, and agriculture, not academia, medicine, engineering, or law. Cameras provided images of boys working in the machine shops, plowing fields, and building sidewalks. Sherman intended boys and girls to be useful laborers within the growing nation, the product of an education provided by a grateful nation to "uncivilized" young people that some considered members of a Vanishing Race. But the camera did not capture vanishing or vanquished Native Americans. Quite the contrary. Images from Sherman Institute portray vibrant, vital, and energetic school children surviving Sherman

and making the best of their situations. The camera captured the next generation of leaders from among the Indian tribes of the United States, young men and women who would lead their people with a better understanding of English and the American system of education, law, and government.

Each photograph depicts a moment in time when these American Indian students lived at Sherman or worked in the Outing Program off campus, making their way in the world and moving forward with their lives in a new setting. Sherman Institute began as an institution dominated by non-Indians determined to assimilate and civilize Native American children, but the institution evolved into an Indian school controlled primarily by Native Americans and dedicated to the preservation of American Indian people, cultures, and languages. Although government officials, administrators, and teachers took the first photographs of Sherman Institute, in time, students used their own cameras to take photographs to remember dances, band concerts, weddings, parades, and other events important to Indian students. Former students donated some photographs found today in the Sherman Collection. These photographs are found herein since some of them are part of the collection found at the Sherman Indian Museum.

As readers enter into this volume, the authors ask you to join in the critical interpretation of each image and consider the shadows behind each photograph. What can the viewer see and what cannot be seen in viewing each image? Who took the photograph and who or what is the subject? When was this photograph taken and why did the photographer select this particular composition? Where was this picture taken? Was the photographer on campus, at the school farm, or away from school walls within the larger community of Southern California? Why was this photograph taken? What was the purpose of this photograph, and did the photographer have something in mind to convey to viewers? And what did the photographer wish to convey? Finally, what is not seen but might be implied given the subject, era, and angle of the photograph?

Seen and unseen shadows of Sherman Institute have influenced generations of Native Americans and their homelands. Sherman Institute has played a role

in the lives of thousands of Native Americans and represents a portion of American history. Established as a genocidal institution, the school altered the lives of multiple generations of Native American students and parents. It also played a significant and weighty role in the lives of school administrators, teachers, and disciplinarians, some of whom were Native Americans and others who were non-Indians. Sherman Institute profoundly influenced the lives of thousands of students as well as many citizens of Riverside who interacted with the school. Sherman Institute had a long-lasting effect on the Native American employees of the school as well as their families, some of who contributed to the creation and interpretation of this present work. Collectively, these individuals and families call themselves Sherman Brats, as they have had a lengthy association with each other and Sherman. Sherman Brats are the children of Native American teachers, coaches, dorm supervisors, grounds keepers, and other indigenous people working at Sherman Institute. Because their parents worked for Sherman, the brats could not attend school at Sherman. Federal law prohibited them from going to school at Sherman, so they attended public or private schools. However, these individuals grew up on the Sherman campus and have the greatest knowledge of Sherman's past, particularly the physical plant. Since Sherman Brats grew up on campus, many contemporary brats have deep personal knowledge of the school's history and change over time.

Today, many Sherman Brats and former employees, students, and members of the Sherman Family volunteer at Sherman Indian museum, serving as docents and consultants. They volunteer to help visitors and scholars—Native and non-Native alike who want to learn from their first-hand knowledge. In recent years, they have trained interns at Sherman Indian Museum and engaged scholars in conversation, sharing their own stories with students of Native American history. Lorene Sisquoc and Galen Townsend are two Sherman Brats, and they both are devoted to sharing the history and culture of Sherman Institute. They have also contributed a great deal to the understanding of the photographic record found in the archives at the Sherman Indian Museum and found in this book. They are responsible for the preservation of Sherman's memory and they care greatly about the well being of the school's mission to advance Indian education.[36]

Since 1902, Sherman has hosted thousands of American Indian students as well as Native faculty and employees interested in working for and with other Native Americans. Their images and the shadows they cast survive through thousands of photographs. Former and current students help us understand the meaning and consequences of the American Indian boarding school experience. The photographs found in this volume provide one way of viewing Sherman's world from roughly 1902 to 1970. The unique images found in volume provide a limited and selective view of one federal off-reservation American Indian boarding school that functioned throughout the twentieth century and remains active today as Sherman Indian High School. The photographs and descriptions offered here present a new and original presentation intended to graphically inform viewers interested in one view of the Indian School on Magnolia Avenue.

...

I.2. Gathered around her children, Rose Lisa Lisalnas (bottom center) poses with her family. All of her children shown here attended Sherman Institute in the early twentieth century. From top, left to right: Cha-Cha, Jessie, Kate, Mararil (Sara); from bottom row, left to right: Sonny, Rose Lisa, and George. Photograph courtesy of Edward D. Castillo. Rose Lisa was Castillo's maternal great-grandmother and Sara was his grandmother.

The Sherman Bulletin

Published weekly as a regular part of the school work of Sherman Institute
Volume XXI Riverside, California, September 23, 1927 Number 2
SHERMAN GROUP RETURN FROM EXTENDED TOUR

Mr. C. W. Cell, religious director, William Lorentino, Martin Napa and Melvin Sidwell, from the greatest program tour ever attempted by a Sherman group. Approximately 200 programs were given while traveling about 10,000 miles in nine western states, in a little over three months time.

The programs were given with the educational and helpful thought in mind for a worthy cause, and that the public generally might better understand the high class of work being done for the Indian youth of America under the leadership and direction of the Indian Bureau, for the academic and vocational training, and by the Christian churches of America for their moral and spiritual uplift. Mr. Cell received many letters and testimonials from prominent organization leaders as to the merit of the programs all along the line and practically all of these gave pressing invitations for a return program at some future time.

The entire group report intensely interesting, and highly educational features connected with the tour. A few of these were recalled and described by Mr. Cell in the two splendid programs put on by the group Saturday and Sunday evening at the school auditorium. The exceptional versatility of the programs was shown by the several different roles that Lorentino and Napa appeared in Saturday evening. Peter Masten and Albert LaRose who were with the group early in the three months tour both gave readings, Melvin Sidwell accompanied on the piano.

Mr. Cell spoke of the Carquinez bridge across the bay at San Francisco, which is a mile in length, as being unsurpassed by anything of its kind in America, and that Seattle is the finest, cleanest city in the west; and that Yellowstone is without a doubt the greatest of natures wonderlands to be found anywhere in the world: and that it is impossible to find words that are suitable to picture the grandeur and beauty of Crater Lake the land of the sky blue waters. But after all the group were unanimous in saying that old Sherman looked the best of all when they returned, and that they would all appreciate it more this year than ever before

•••

CHAPTER ONE

Student Life

Children of all ages attended Sherman Institute, and their experiences at the Indian School on Magnolia Avenue varied widely. Students from five to twenty-five years old left their homes on Indian Reservations found throughout the United States to enroll at Sherman. Some lived at the institute for many years without ever going home, while others periodically left school to spend some time with their families, friends, and communities. Sherman and other off-reservation federal boarding schools aimed at changing the lives of children forever, making them over to create a new "American Indian" that spoke English, valued Christianity, and served a useful purpose to the dominant society as productive laborers. At times, students eagerly entered school, desiring to participate in sports, play in the band, learn a vocation, or join a student club. Others preferred to remain on their reservation or indigenous community where they could live as their ancestors before them. Federal agents, teachers, athletic coaches, and school superintendents worked hard to convince parents and tribal leaders that formal education in the Western sense of the word at the boarding school would prove beneficial for every American Indian child. The efforts of their work varied over time and place. Sometimes parents agreed to send their children to Sherman. Sometimes Indian Superintendents forced indigenous children to leave their parents or grandparents, sending them from their homes in Arizona, New Mexico, Alaska, New York, Oklahoma, North Dakota, Minnesota, Kansas, Washington, Oregon, and many other states and territories to the "Land of Oranges" in Riverside, California. Students that attended Sherman came from many different regions and various tribes of the United States. Students traveled to school by railroad, wagon, automobiles, and buses. In the fall of every year, vehicles pulled onto the curb in front of Sherman, parking temporarily on Magnolia Avenue. Students shuffled heavy luggage onto the sidewalk situated on the north side of the campus. Sherman appeared as an imposing place with its multi-storied buildings, grass, and towering date palm trees that contrasted significantly against the deep blue sky hanging over Sherman. Once students arrived, doctors and nurses checked them for "defects" and infectious diseases, which they might spread to members of the student body, faculty, staff, and administration. School employees took the clothing from every child, cut their hair, had them shower, and deloused them to kill lice and identify students with scabies. Medical people weighed students to record and monitor their weight, one indication that the student had contracted tuberculosis.

Life for students at Sherman Institute proved difficult, often frightening, for students. Many students suffered from homesickness and depression. Some students adjusted to homesickness and others did not. Some students hated their boarding school experience and others enjoyed it. Student views varied widely and still do. No one assessment of the boarding schools exists as each student had a different experience. Conditions and situations at the school and student attitudes toward Sherman changed over time, but the fact remains, young Native American students found it difficult to adjust to life away from home and away from their parents, grandparents, and community elders. But many students learned to "turn the power" on an institution and body of school officials determined to assimilate indigenous children. Non-Native policy makers had established Sherman Institute to destroy American Indian cultures, languages, and religions. Students used their boarding school experiences to support, preserve, and protect indigenous cultures and to benefit their people. Students learned English and the cultural, political, and economic ways of mainstream Americans. Students participated in student government, joined student clubs, joined in sport programs, learned to play new music and musical instruments, became proficient in trades, and found meaningful employment through Sherman to earn money to support their families back on the reservations. Some students moved to town where they used their skills to benefit themselves and their families. Each student experienced Sherman differently, but Sherman changed the lives of every student in numerous ways. Sometimes the images found here speak to the change in student life over time. Many photographs exist in the photographic collection of Sherman Indian Museum that depict elements of student life. Many images show students enjoying their experiences. However, it is unlikely that photographers would have sought out unhappy, depressed, or discontented children to photograph as their subjects. Photographs of homesick, tearful Indian children on campus would not have been in keeping with the upbeat, positive impression desired by those creating the photographic compositions of student life at Sherman Institute.

•••

> *"Each student experienced Sherman differently, but Sherman changed the lives of every student in numerous ways."*

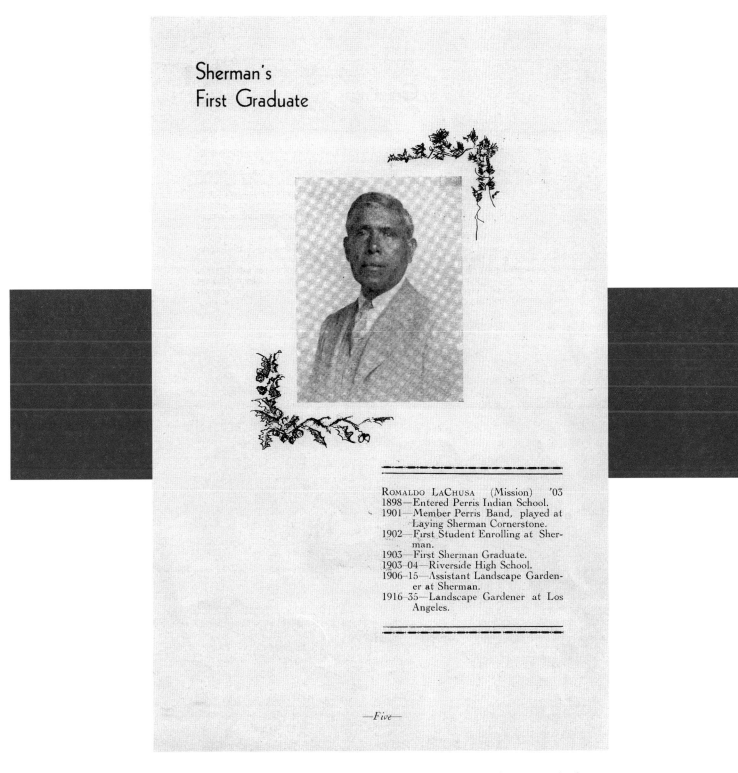

Sherman's
First Graduate

ROMALDO LaCHUSA (Mission) '03
1898—Entered Perris Indian School.
1901—Member Perris Band, played at
Laying Sherman Cornerstone.
1902—First Student Enrolling at Sherman.
1903—First Sherman Graduate.
1903–04—Riverside High School.
1906–15—Assistant Landscape Gardener at Sherman.
1916–35—Landscape Gardener at Los
Angeles.

—Five—

1.1. Romaldo La Chusa enrolled in Sherman Institute in 1902, becoming the first student to attend the Indian School on Magnolia Avenue. Because of his earlier schooling at the Perris Indian School, La Chusa also became the first student to graduate from Sherman Institute a year later in 1903. La Chusa combined the vocational training and post graduation work experience he received at Sherman to become a successful landscaper in Los Angeles, California.

1.2. Students arrived at Sherman Institute via many different modes of transportation, including, horses, buggies, wagons, trolleys, trains, and automobiles. This photograph depicts students arriving at school in buses parked off Magnolia Avenue, which runs in front of Sherman Institute and was one of the first divided thoroughfares in California. Most Native American students arrived from rural reservation homes where the built environments were minimal with little or no automobile traffic. The site of Sherman Institute and all the buildings of Riverside must have been impressive and intimidating for many new students.

1.3. Ida Gooday Largo, a Chiricahua Apache and relative of Mangus Coloradas, was born in Indian Territory as a prisoner of war. Her father had fought with Geronimo and was among the last Apache warriors to surrender to Lieutenant Charles Gatewood in 1886. Ida attended federal Indian boarding schools and became a strict teacher. She worked at the boarding school at Tuba City, Arizona, on the Navajo Reservation before teaching at Sherman Institute. She raised her children on campus, thereby becoming members of a unique group of people known as the Sherman Brats. In this photograph, Mrs. Largo stands and instructs Sherman students on the proper way to do appliqué using indigenous designs. Ida Gooday Largo was the mother of Tonita Largo, and grandmother of Lorene Sisquoc (not pictured), Curator of the Sherman Indian School Museum and co-editor of this volume.

1.4. "Indian Children Taught by Indian Teachers." From the outset, some of the teachers at Sherman Institute were Native Americans that worked for the Office of Indian Education. In this photograph, the teacher has divided students into two groups. The teacher on the left is providing a storytelling session to boys and girls. The teacher has also composed a sentence on the board to the right that lacks some words. The boy at the chalkboard is providing the missing words. Notice the boy's military boots and spats. Also, above the blackboard is a calendar depicting a tribal elder and a child, teaching in the old way through the oral tradition. The curriculum at Sherman Institute included many subjects, including writing and storytelling. Most students were raised in their oral tradition. Learning to speak and write in the English language offered a daunting challenge for students. But Sherman students developed their language skills, and many learned to speak, read, and write English at a high level.

1.5. Five boys and one girl in a science class prepare to take a timed examination. Notice that the teacher standing in the background holds a stopwatch in his left hand. The photograph speaks to issues of time. Native American concepts of time differed greatly from most non-Native Americans. School officials did not like or use the concept of "Indian Time," and they emphasized punctuality to promote assimilation and the work ethic.

1.6. Women students at Sherman Institute received many courses of study in Domestic Science, commonly called Home Economics. This photograph provides a staged picture of Sherman women engaged in a class on Baby Sitting. The class is seen here engaged in reading Mary Furlong Moore's volume, *The Baby Sitter's Guide*. In addition to classroom teaching about baby sitting and baby care, young Sherman women took practicums where they worked with baby dolls and the children of employees at Sherman Institute at a daycare center on campus.

1.7. [Left] Harwood Hall spent his life working for the Office of Indian Affairs. He was a disciple of Richard Henry Pratt, the architect of off-reservation American Indian boarding schools and superintendent of Carlisle Indian Industrial School in Pennsylvania. Before becoming the first superintendent at Sherman, Hall served as an Indian agent and superintendent of the Phoenix Indian School and Perris Indian School. During his tenure at Perris, Superintendent Hall convinced Congressman James Sherman of the need for a new Indian school given the poor water supply at Perris. In the fall of 1902, Hall became the first Superintendent of Sherman Institute in Riverside, California when the new school opened with eight grade levels.

1.8. [Right] Frances D. Hall, the wife of Harwood Hall, came to Sherman Institute in 1902. Over the course of many years, she was involved with students and worked as an employee of the Office of Indian Affairs but not at Sherman while Harwood was superintendent. When she moved to Sherman in 1902, Frances served as the "First Lady" of Sherman Institute and set up the superintendent's home, furnishing it, in part, with a beautiful collection of Southern California Native American baskets. Some students regarded Mr. and Mrs. Hall "parents" who showed them kindness. Others disliked the Halls because of their paternalism and their power over children. Later, the Hall family donated their baskets to the precursor of the Riverside Metropolitan Museum, which possesses one of the largest collections of Native American basketry in California.

1.9. Sherman Institute offered a gendered curriculum, in which most girls learned to sew. Here girls were sewing clothing with foot powered treadle sewing machines. Many female students went on to become successful seamstresses both on and off Indian reservations. Learning to sew remained part of the gendered curriculum at Sherman throughout most of the twentieth century, but Sherman girls also took classes in the Domestic Sciences that included caring for children, cooking, cleaning, and first aid. Notice the girl in the background ironing her project.

1.10. In the early twentieth century, Sherman girls learned to use treadle sewing machines powered with their feet. However, after the 1940s, female students learned to use modern sewing machines powered by electricity. Nevertheless, female students who returned to work as seamstresses on Indian reservations most likely continued to use the treadle sewing machines as most reservations did not have electricity at the time. Learning to sew was a major focus of Home Economics at Sherman and provided a skill used by women on reservations. Many Native American women made their own clothing for themselves and their families. One former Sherman student remembered her family making alterations to clothing on the San Manuel Indian Reservation. They also altered clothing donated to reservation families from local churches and other relief agencies serving the poor.

1.11. During her years at Sherman Institute, photographers occasionally took pictures of students and gave a copy to the student. This is a candid photograph of Margarita Lisalda dressed in a handmade dress which she had constructed in a sewing class. Photo courtesy of Edward D. Castillo.

1.12. Sherman Institute encouraged females to learn how to sew. In addition to washing and drying clothing, girls made and repaired bed linens. Students depicted in this photograph were using sewing machines to make or repair sheets, and pillowcases for their fellow Sherman students. Students commonly provided services for other students at Sherman, which the administration believed helped students build skills and a sense of community on campus. Student labor also kept administrative costs down.

1.13. This photograph depicts a portion of the laundry at Sherman Institute where boys and girls worked every day but Sundays as part of their educations. Note the large laundry tumblers and the adjacent ironing stations to the left. Boys helped lift the heavier clothes into the washing machines. Boys and girls worked together to load and run bulky laundry tumblers, but female students alone performed the ironing, a hot and tedious task before the invention of air conditioning.

1.14. Girls at Sherman Institute took many courses in Home Economics. At the Perris Indian School and Sherman Institute, girls did the ironing for the entire school population. In the early twentieth century, girls heated their irons on wood or coal burning stoves, moving their heavy metal irons from hot stoves to ironing boards. These girls ironed clothing using electrical irons. Female students trained in the use of electric irons for the purposes of employment and assimilation into life off reservations, as many reservations were without electricity. Whether using the old style of irons or newer electrical irons, Sherman females ironed sheets, dresses, shirts, pants, towels, and other articles common on campus.

1.15. Sherman Institute boasted a large laundry operation that included eighteen ironing stations. As part of their work on campus, female students ironed clothing and sheets for the entire student body. As part of the assimilation process, administrators prided themselves on having Sherman students dress in clean neat non-Native clothing. Ironing was also part of the school's program to teach students to be sanitary, neat, and clean. For Christian reformers, cleanliness was close to godliness, an image school officials wanted students to project on and off campus.

1.16. Girls at Sherman Institute learned to make quilts as part of the Domestic Science curriculum. Many Sherman girls returned home to reservations to use their skills as quilters to make beautiful and useful quilted blankets for their families, friends, and relatives. Some indigenous quilters became famous by using Native American themes and designs in their quilts, like the famous Star Design of Cherokee and other tribal people. Note the use of non-Native motifs and patterns in the quilt. However, despite not being encouraged to create traditional Native blankets, students at Sherman used traditional knowledge of design to make new quilting styles.

1.17. [Above] Margarita Lisalda majored in Domestic Science at Sherman Institute and attended classes with the same cohort shown in this group photograph in a kitchen at the Indian boarding school. To remember her classmates, Margarita wrote the name of every girl in her class above her image. Most of the names have faded with time, but many students kept photographs of their boarding school days at the Indian school on Magnolia Avenue.

1.18. [Below] This is a very rare photograph of a certificate of completion given to students at graduation ceremonies. No copy of a certificate exists at the National Archives or at Sherman Indian Museum. This copy is courtesy of Edward D. Castillo.

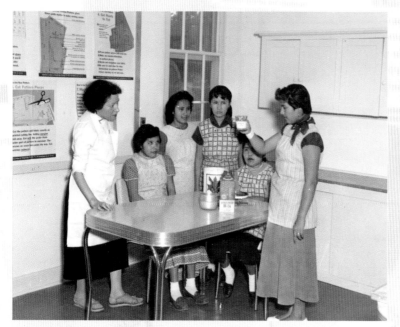

1.19. As part of their training in Domestic Science, female students learned to measure ingredients as part of the cooking curriculum. This photograph depicts students learning how to cook with cow's milk, an ingredient not found in traditional Native American cuisine. For the most part, boys learned to be chefs and cook for larger numbers of people. Sherman girls learned to cook for families and smaller groups. The curriculum in Domestic Sciences taught females to prepare to be good wives or competent maids and babysitters for families.

1.20. Sherman girls learned to cook for families and small groups. As part of their limited curriculum, Sherman girls prepared to become housewives or domestics for non-Native families. Many Sherman females worked off campus in the Outing Program. The school encouraged them to live in the homes of non-Indian families where they cooked for the families of their employers. The girls depicted in this photograph are rolling out pie crust and preparing fruit filling to make a pie. Sherman cooking classes almost exclusively advocated a western diet, despite being nutritionally inferior to Native foods and detrimental to Native people's long-term health. However, the Western diet followed the rationale of school officials who wished to assimilate students through the curriculum and work experience.

1.21. In Home Economics classes at Sherman Institute, female students learned to mix dough and bake bread. Note to the right in the photograph the stovepipe coming from the wood-burning oven, an essential tool in cooking on and off the reservation for generations. For those students returning home to reservations, they often found that the skills they had learned at school could not be replicated at home due to the lack of equipment, such as modern stoves.

1.22. These young women at Sherman Institute cooked on a wood-burning stove as part of their curriculum in Domestic Science. At Sherman, instructors did not teach reservation-bound girls to cook outdoors over an open fire or in a small fireplace in the homes of many students. School officials taught students "modern" techniques of cooking as part of the attempt to assimilate young girls. Teachers at Sherman taught girls to be part of the domestic sphere of a non-reservation house where girls might find permanent employment as servants, which was a common profession for Native American women living during the early twentieth century.

CHAPTER TWO

Student Education

Superintendents, teachers, and dorm assistants at Sherman Institute took many photographs of students at work and learning vocations. Like all the off-reservation American Indian boarding schools, Sherman Institute was first and foremost an industrial school that taught boys and girls trades and agriculture. Students at Sherman could learn from a variety of trades, especially boys who had far more career choices than girls. The limited curriculum for females at Sherman Institute and other Indian schools mirrored the larger dominant society that limited opportunities for females in the United States between 1900 and 1970. Leaders of the Office of Indian Education believed the Indian schools should train girls in the domestic sphere. Thus, the curriculum at Sherman Institute taught Native American girls to be good mothers, maids, governesses, baby sitters, and chambermaids. Sherman's curriculum for females emphasized home economics or domestic sciences for girls. As part of their practical work curriculum at Sherman Institute, images at the Sherman Indian Museum show girls washing, ironing, sewing, mending, and cooking. Numerous photographs exist depicting girls learning to be nurses, tending small children, sewing dresses, measuring ingredients for baking, and working as student beauticians. School officials purposely limited educational opportunities for girls at Sherman, reflecting the male orientation of American society during most of the twentieth century.

The Outing Program at Sherman Institute originally provided more opportunities for girls than boys. School superintendents found that the general public beyond the school walls wanted Indian girls to work in their homes more than they wanted boys. As a result, Sherman girls often left school to work in the homes of non-Indians in several cities and towns in Southern California, including Los Angeles, Riverside, Fontana, Hemet, San Diego, and San Bernardino. A great demand existed for Sherman females to work within the homes in the area where the Outing student took care of the home as a live-in maid, babysitter, cook, and cleaner. For the most part, school officials did not often oversee these girls but remained in touch with them to monitor their behavior and that of their hosts. Sherman girls also found employment as hotel maids, cooks, and kitchen workers, helping out at several establishments, including the famous Mission Inn. Several girls enjoyed being away from home and school, living an independent life in urban areas far from the reservation. Often, Sherman Institution served as an employment agency for Native American girls and boys who worked for families and businesses.

Boys clearly had more curricular and employment opportunities than girls. The curriculum for boys at Sherman centered on the industrial arts and agriculture. Photographs at Sherman Indian Museum illustrate this fact and show changes in job opportunities over time. Vocational education for boys changed over time, and the photographs capture this dramatic change. For example, in the early twentieth century, Sherman Institute offered boys a curriculum and career opportunities in such trades as those producing wheelwrights, harness makers, cobblers, blacksmiths, and other fields associated with leather works, wagons, and horses. From roughly 1900 to 1920, the curriculum for boys reflected class offerings in these fields, but advances in the automobile industry and mechanized tool technology changed things for Sherman. In the 1920s, Sherman's curriculum dropped these and other fields of study to emphasize curriculum and careers for boys as automobile mechanics, carpenters, welders, and machinists.

Thus, curriculum offerings and work experiences changed over time as some fields disappeared and others emerged, firmly placing Sherman's curriculum in the modern world of the budding twentieth century. In short, photographs depict modernity as Sherman boys walked away from plows pulled by mules to noisy tractors that spew out fumes as they chugged along in the fields of the Sherman farm. As the twentieth century progressed and the United States moved firmly into the

> **"School officials purposely limited educational opportunities for girls at Sherman, reflecting the male orientation of American society during most of the twentieth century."**

modern era, curriculum changed at the boarding schools. This change created problems for Indian students returning to their homelands, sites where modernity was slow in developing. For example, in 1920 on the Hopi Indian Reservation of Northern Arizona, farmers still used digging sticks to cultivate their corn, not tractors, plows, and seeders. A Hopi boy returning home knew how to operate modern farm equipment, but none existed on the reservation. The frustration of a young Hopi student returning home must have been repeated again and again as students trained to use modern equipment but found their reservations lacking in equipment and capital to buy tractors, washing machines, vacuums, ovens, ranges, and automobiles. Over time, Sherman offered boys a curriculum that included automobile mechanics, masonry, machine shop work, welding, barbering, carpentry, cooking, and concrete construction. As part of their curriculum and work on campus, boys learned to build homes, manage electricity, and the art of plumbing. Girls helped cultivate, plant, weed, and harvest truck gardens.

Sherman Boys worked at the school farm, located five miles from the main campus off Indiana Avenue adjacent the Gage Canal. At school and at the farm, Sherman boys received practical knowledge of modern agriculture. Boys learned to drive tractors and operate a variety of farm equipment, which could be dangerous. Boys learned to plow fields and create furrows to

2.1. Sherman Institute offered a gendered curriculum with far more opportunities for boys than girls. This photograph depicts an all-male classroom scene. The school privileged male students, which was common throughout the educational institutions of the early twentieth century. Sherman boys could take a variety of coursework in many fields of study. Although female students did not have as many career opportunities as males, they took some courses together. However, administrators restricted female entrance into several courses, particularly shop classes. In like fashion, male students were prohibited from taking home economics or domestic science classes.

plant with a variety of seeds. The Sherman farms, dairies, and gardens produced an abundance of food for consumption by students and the public alike. Sherman Institute sponsored the production of many crops at the large farm, which school officials used to feed the students and farm animals. Boys at the school farm grew fruits, vegetables, grains, and hay, which the boys fed to beef and dairy cattle. The Sherman dairy produced milk, cheese, and other dairy products for use at Sherman Institute. Sherman superintendents sold excess produce, dairy, beef, pork, poultry, eggs, and other products to Riverside businesses. Several photographs exist depicting agriculture, dairy, gardening, and industrial arts at Sherman Institute.

Photographs at Sherman Indian Museum depict boys and girls learning many trades and the domestic sciences. The museum contains a large body of photographs that document the work-curriculum at Sherman Institute and students actually engaged in work—on and off campus. These images demonstrate that

students were productive and useful, accomplishing tasks common during the era of the early twentieth century. Earlier photographs of males at Sherman indicate classes in leather crafts, harness making, wagon construction, and the creation of wooden wheels. Later photographs show male students at Sherman working as automobile mechanics, welders, masons, carpenters, chefs, barbers, and a host of other trades. Several photographs depict female students sewing, ironing, washing, cooking, and childcare. However, a fair number of photographs taken in the early twentieth century focus on Sherman girls training to be nurses.

When Sherman first opened, Dr. Mary Israel, a medical doctor from England, served as the lead teacher of the nursing program and played a major role at the Sherman hospital where her nursing students received hands on work as nurses.

•••

AMERICAN INDIAN YOUTH TRAINED

for

Productive Employment

at

SHERMAN INSTITUTE

———— • ————

Boys Trained in:

   Carpentry and Mill-Cabinet
      Cooking and Baking
         Machine Shop and Welding
            Painting and Furniture Finishing
               Printing

Girls Trained in:

   Home Service
      General Service
         Power Sewing

———— • ————

SHERMAN INSTITUTE
RIVERSIDE, CALIFORNIA

2.2. [Left] "PRODUCTIVE EMPLOYMENT AT SHERMAN INSTITUTE." Sherman Institute produced a pamphlet announcing employment opportunities for boys and girls. This photograph depicts the school pamphlet listing opportunities for boys: Carpentry, Milled Cabinet Making, Cooking, Baking, Machine Shop, Welding, Painting, Furniture Finishing, and Printing. Sherman Girls could train in Home Service, General Service, and Power Sewing. Note that female students were largely trained in Domestic Sciences to become mothers, maids, childcare providers, domestics, and seamstresses. Sherman females found they could use elements of their educations back on their reservations, but others found they had been taught to use equipment not available on reservations.

2.3. [Below] Every day of the year, Sherman students prepared food for the entire student body. Students ate three meals each day, and students worked continually to serve food to each other. This photograph depicts boys making biscuits or rolls to serve to their fellow students. Boys at Sherman Institute could take a course of study to become bakers. This was not a vocational option for girls. Many Sherman graduates went on to work in some of the best restaurants and eateries throughout the American Southwest, including the Mission Inn in Riverside, California.

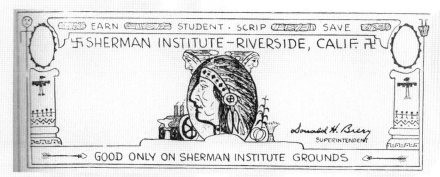

2.4. [Left] Sherman Institute made scrip that students could "earn" and "save" to use on campus. The Sherman Scrip read: "Good Only On Sherman Institute Grounds." Since Sherman Scrip could not be used off campus, students had to use money sent from home or earned from the Outing Program if they wished to buy anything away from campus. School students used Sherman Scrip to purchase small items on campus, such as paper, pencils, and postcards. Note the Native motifs incorporated into the currency's design. These stylistic choices included two bent crosses that should not be mistaken as a Nazi swastika, but ancient designs used by Native peoples long before Nazism claimed the symbol in the mid-twentieth century.

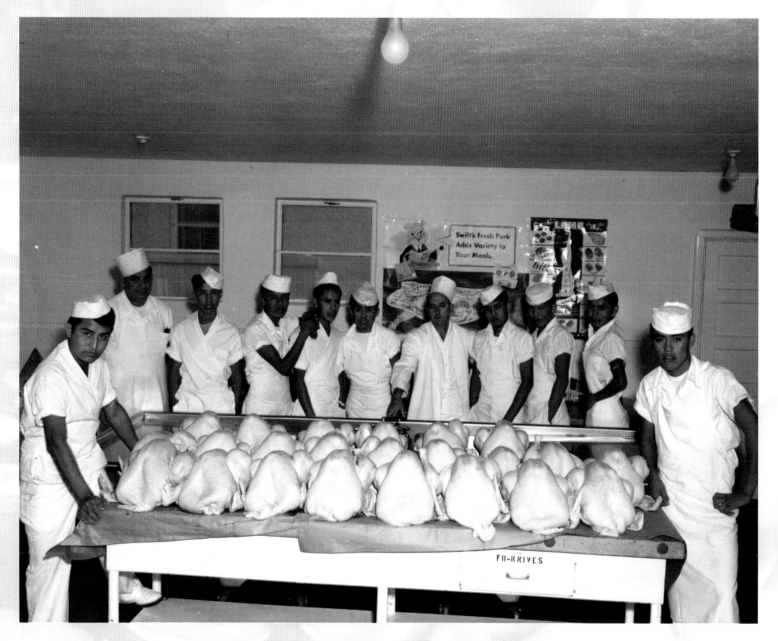

2.5. Sherman officials encouraged the celebration of holidays known throughout America in the twentieth century. Students depicted in this photograph prepare for either Thanksgiving or Christmas dinner. They prepare to cook several turkeys, for dinner at Sherman Institute. As a way to introduce students to and encourage them to adopt non-Native cultural customs, students at Sherman often prepared traditional holiday meals for their fellow students like roasted turkey.

2.6. Both boys and girls learned to cook at Sherman Institute. Sherman men learned to cook for large groups, while women cooked for families. These boys are making pancakes to be served to other students in the school cafeteria. As part of the Sherman curriculum, school officials taught boys to be short order cooks and chefs. They taught girls to cook for families, expecting them to remain in the domestic sphere either in their own homes or those of non-Indians who hired young Sherman women to work as live-in maids. Note how cooking classes for men tended to prepare them for employment in the culinary field whereas female students Domestic Science courses were geared towards preparing women as wives and maids.

2.7. In the early twentieth century, Sherman offered a course of study for boys to become wheelwrights, a specialized field to make wooden wheels for wagons, buggies, and hacks. Notice the blacksmith forge and anvils on the left, used for courses in these two disciplines. When Sherman opened its doors in 1902, the automobile industry was in its infancy. Most Americans, including indigenous people, still used wagon for transportation, but this fact changed as the century progressed. With time, the curriculum at Sherman modernized. As buggies gave way to automobiles, Sherman offered classes in automotive technology.

2.8. [Left] Male students at Sherman Institute could learn to be blacksmiths or metalworkers. Like the trade of training wheelwrights, Sherman changed its curriculum over time from blacksmithing to metal-working. Sherman boys could learn to weld metals with modern equipment and create numerous projects with metals that improved their skills and enhanced the campus. As part of the curriculum, Sherman males worked on campus on many construction projects, including those that required metalworking.

2.9. [Below] Sherman Institute boasted its own machine shops where boys learned a specialized trade. In machine shops, Sherman boys learned to make many kinds of parts used to replace broken or worn out elements of equipment used on campus. The students made new parts for the motor seen on the front table. Machinists were in great demand in factories found within urban areas. School officials encouraged boys to learn to be machinists and take positions in the cities of America. Reservations provided few opportunities for machinists. Thus, this field of study fit into the assimilation program of the school to encourage students to become part of mainstream America.

2.10. From 1901 forward, Sherman boys worked on campus to frame school buildings and learn techniques of carpentry and home building. At Sherman Institute, boys could study different forms of carpentry and learn to build barns, homes, and smaller projects like the cow feeder depicted in this photograph. Carpentry courses prepared Sherman students to work in the construction industry that witnesses a tremendous boom in the California and the American West, particularly after World War I and World War II.

2.11. Some Sherman male students learned the art of printing, an important skill enabling them to find work in several industries. At Sherman, printing students produced the Sherman Bulletin, the school newspaper, annual, pamphlets, and books. Sherman boys sometimes found work in shops throughout the nation. Sherman boys received practical experience in the printing business. In this photograph, notice the four printing presses and a tray of type.

OLD FIRE CIRCLE

2.12. "The Old Fire Circle" offered a central gathering place for Sherman students. According to Sherman historian Galen Townsend, only the boys and girls attending Sherman Institute (and some Sherman Brats) could attend student functions held at the Fire Circle. Sherman students met at the Fire Circles to enjoy picnics. Notice the stonework. Sherman students learned how to do stone masonry, and they would meet at this popular gathering place to build fires, sing songs, and eat snacks.

2.13. [Left] Some Sherman students took courses of study in commercial painting. The boy in this photograph uses an electrical sprayer to paint a wicker chair with an air-powered spray gun. Wicker furniture became popular in the United States in the twentieth century. For some people the furniture was more breathable than solid wood or upholstered furniture. The woven nature of wicker furniture lent itself to the Arts & Crafts movement and provided additional opportunities for Sherman students that included the creation and repairing of wicker furniture.

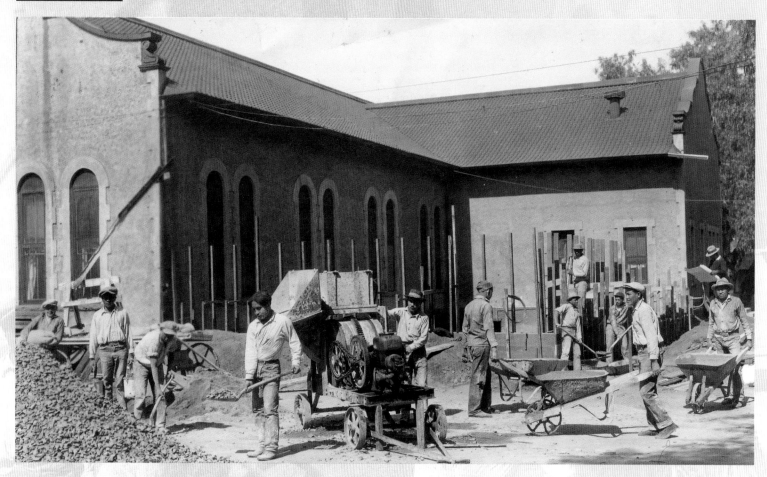

2.14. [Below] As part of the curriculum and work program of Sherman Institute, superintendents assigned students to build and repair buildings, sidewalks, and retaining walls. This photograph depicts students mixing and spreading cement. Note the old cement mixer and use of wheelbarrows. Rock and sand appear in the photograph as well, ready to be used to mix with cement. Vocational courses at Sherman Institute included classes on masonry. In 1901, Sherman boys that had studied masonry at the Perris Indian School used their skills working with construction crews to build structures at the Indian School on Magnolia Avenue. This photograph depicts students at Sherman in the process of building an addition to an existing structure designed in the Mission Revival style.

2.15. Vocational painting courses at Sherman Institute taught male students to paint with rollers, brushes, and paint sprayers. Students painted smaller projects, including furniture, but they also took on much larger projects, including the painting of buildings and classrooms on the Sherman campus. Note that these students are using white paint as an aesthetic nod to the whitewash finish commonly applied to the finish on adobe buildings in Spanish missions of California.

2.16. This photograph depicts Sherman students painting a dormitory on the Sherman campus. Note the students used scaffolding in order to paint the upper stories of the building. Keeping the buildings and physical environment at Sherman clean and in pristine order was important to the administrators and educators at Sherman. School officials and those of the Office of Indian Affairs often viewed Indian life on Indian reservations as unclean and disheveled. Sherman superintendents sought to create a clean and orderly campus to teach students new values championed in the dominant society.

Greetings

To Graduates and Students
of Sherman Institute:

This is a word of **greeting** to you. I believe you are in a fortunate position. You have had or are acquiring education and training which will make you especially fitted to assume responsibilities in Indian matters among your own people. Opportunities are now available for the Indians of the various jurisdictions and in their various communities to assume real leadership in the development of their affairs.

Opportunities for earning a livelihood are greater than ever before in connection with the wider and better use of Indian lands, in occupations connected with the development of Indian life, and in Indian organizations.

Each one of you should look forward to the acquisition of full information relative to the opportunities and to making yourselves a right-thinking and integral part of the new possibilities. You must use your own intelligence, supplemented by your education and experiences, You must not be misled by those who have merely their own interests to promote. Together in groups, you should discuss your affairs and help develop the best that the future may hold.

My good wishes are with you.

JOHN COLLIER
Commissioner

May 10, 1935.

2.17. "GREETINGS TO GRADUATES AND STUDENTS OF SHERMAN INSTITUTE." During the Great Depression, Commissioner of Indian Affairs John Collier wrote the students at Sherman on May 10, 1936, informing them of the "fortunate position" they found themselves in at Sherman. According to Collier, Sherman students were to use their "own intelligence" along with the "education and experiences" at Sherman so that these students could "assume real leadership in the development of their [Indian] affairs." However, Collier also added a note of caution that students must be "right-thinking" so that they will "not be misled by those who have merely their own interests to promote."

2.18. At Sherman, students learned to care for domesticated ducks on the Sherman farm. School officials situated ducks and other foul a short distance south of campus. Students learned to care for ducks, turkeys, and chickens. Students worked through the Outing Program on local farms that raised ducks, geese, turkeys, and chickens. Poultry farms hosted Sherman students who worked for less money than other farm laborers.

2.19. Sherman boys also raised and tended a modern and extensive dairy. Twice a day, Sherman students milked the cows at the Sherman dairy. Sherman boys also raised beef cattle for meat eaten by students and sold to local businesses. This photograph depicts a number of boys tying down an animal for a procedure, not to harm the animal. Sometimes boys tied down cows to tag their ears with identification numbers or brand them, showing the school owned the cow. The boy on the left holds an ominous looking tool the boys may have used to assist the cow. Beef cattle and dairy cattle supported the student population at Sherman, providing meat and milk.

2.20. This photograph depicts a sow at Sherman Institute that lived in the hog barns located on the main campus south of the administration, dorms, and Main Building. The picture shows thirteen tiny piglets nursing their mother. Boys tended the hog farm on the Sherman campus, and the animals brought roasts, ribs, bacon, and hams to the Sherman cafeteria to be eaten by students. Tending hogs played a role in the curriculum of Sherman. In addition to helping in the birthing, raising, and feeding of hogs every day, boys also learned how to butcher the animals. School administrators sold surplus pork to local markets. Students involved in the raising of these pigs received a portion of the sale proceeds as payment for their labor in Sherman Scrip.

2.21. The photographer took this picture at the Sherman Farm located about five miles from the main campus on Indiana Avenue in Riverside, California. Two horses are shown pulling the plow controlled by a Sherman student. Notice the distinctive water tower in the background. When Sherman Institute opened in 1902, boys learned to plow fields with teams of horses and mules. At the Sherman farm located southwest of campus, Sherman boys walked behind plows pulled by draft animals. However, as time passed into the twentieth century, school officials bought tractors that students operated. In addition, students learned to use various forms of farm equipment, which greatly enhanced the production found at the Sherman farm.

2.22. Many boys at Sherman Institute learned to operate tractors and other farm equipment. A photographer took this picture in the 1930s with the water tower in the background. Sherman boys and men used their agricultural skills, including their ability to operate farm machinery, when they found work through the Outing Program. However, when students returned home to their reservations they found that indigenous people had not participated in modernity. Few tractors and farm equipment existed on most Indian reservations until well into the twentieth century. Many Indians managed their farms with hand tools, including wooden digging sticks.

2.23. Two Sherman boys tend to chickens housed in a coup located on the main campus of Sherman Institute. From 1902 forward, Sherman supported chicken coups filled with animals that laid dozens of eggs each day. The school used the eggs for numerous meals for Indian students. Cooks used eggs for baking and put egg into foods and drinks. Every child at Sherman had several jobs, and administrators had assigned these boys to feed the chickens and pick up the eggs each morning. When chickens stopped laying eggs, these boys would butcher and pluck them for fried or baked chicken, chicken soup, and many other dishes.

Tepee Garden

2.24. Each dormitory on the campus of Sherman Institute had its own garden. Girls from the Tepee Dormitory prepare the soil of their garden with the help of a male instructor. The gardens were intended to teach healthy living and self-reliance through western gardening practices that often eschewed indigenous farming techniques that did not conform to non-Native ideas of symmetry and mastery of nature. Probably staged, the students in the photograph appear to be dressed more appropriately for work inside as opposed to outside in a garden.

2.25. This photograph was taken in one of the many packinghouses for citrus established in Riverside, California. Sunkist owned this particular packinghouse, and they regularly hired Sherman men and women to work on the shed during harvest season. The vast majority of students at Sherman Institute participated in the Outing Program. Although some students worked in the trades, most worked on ranches, picked fruit, and labored in the agricultural sector. Sherman students also worked in packing sheds, especially in Riverside where Sunkist and other companies hired Sherman boys and girls to pack citrus. This photograph is of students inside a Sunkist naval orange packing facility. Citrus was big business for much of the twentieth century in Southern California, and Sherman students worked in all facets of the fruits cultivation.

2.26. This rare photograph depicts four young Sherman men working on the electrical lines leading into the dairy. These boys, training in electrical work, attend to the electrical lines sending electrical energy to the dairy barn and ancillary buildings associated with the dairy at Sherman Institute. The school supported a modern dairy, including electric lights and, at a later date, milking machines to help students. Work on electricity led some Sherman men to find work in electronics. They often found temporary work as laborers and linesmen, fixing electrical and telephone lines. While some of them worked off Sherman's campus, others worked in the Outing Program as electricians. After learning basics about electricity on campus, they found an additional education and on-the-job experience through the Outing Program.

2.27. During the fire season, generally during the summer months in Southern California, the United States Forest Service trained and employed male students from Sherman to help fight fires. These boys worked for the Oak Grove division of Angeles National Forest and took the name, Sherman Hot Shots. Sherman men became well known as brave and efficient fire fighters throughout the forests of San Diego, San Bernardino, Orange, Los Angeles, Riverside, and other nearby counties for their skills as fire fighters. Note that this photograph of Sherman Hot Shots was taken while the students were working in the Los Angeles National Forest. Sherman students fought fires in the National Forests of Southern California that equaled over one million acres. The forests of Southern California vary drastically in climate, topography, elevation, and environment in a region known primarily for the Pacific Coast.

2.28. For many Sherman students, the quality, upkeep, and style of their hair provided them with a measure of pride and honor. At Sherman, all students had to keep their hair short. Sherman students learned to work as barbers and hairdressers. Some female students at Sherman learned to be hairdressers. Male students could take a course of study to become barbers. Perhaps as another way to encourage Native students to cut their hair short, Sherman students learned how to cut hair by practicing on each other. The small sign on the door in the upper portion of the photograph reads, "Work done by students exclusively."

2.29. [Left] Some female students took cosmetology classes at Sherman Institute to be hairdressers. This photograph from the collections of Sherman Indian Museum depicts a Sherman student having her hair dried with a modern manner at the school salon. The Sherman student dries her hair in a new style dryer. This form of hairdressing provided Sherman girls a new and luxurious form of hair care. However, many reservations did not have beauty parlors until the end of the twentieth century.

2.30. [Below] In the 1950s, Sherman Institute began new programs in cosmetology. These programs were strictly the domain of female students and offered a new and exciting field of study for Sherman females. Girls learned to offer pedicures and manicures. They learned to cut, perm, and style hair. Similar to male students in the barber program, female students at Sherman Institute practiced on their fellow students before seeking employment outside of the Indian School on Magnolia Avenue. This photograph depicts one Sherman student giving another student a manicure.

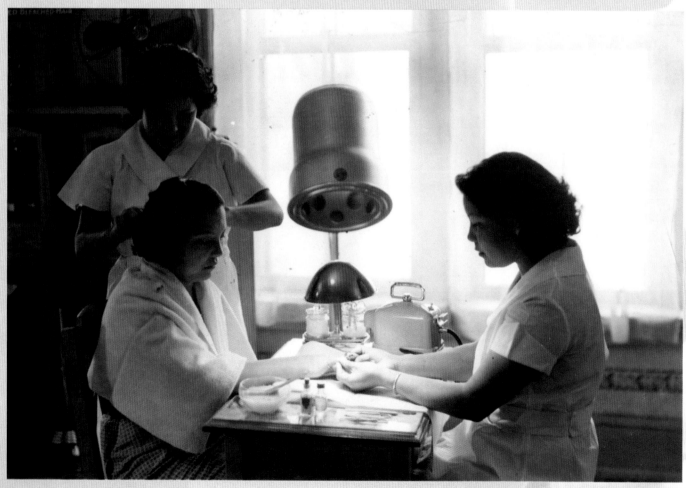

2.31. This is a staged photograph of an employer or homemaker demonstrating the use of her vacuum to a young Sherman woman working in a home or business. The girl likely needs no such instruction but the photographer wanted an image of a girl on an Outing. Sherman students participating in the Outing Program were in a tenuous position. They were not in charge of their living circumstances or the kind of people for whom they worked. Many Sherman Outing students enjoyed their experiences, but others complained about their situations. Some students had to deal with racism and paternalism with some non-Indians treating the Indian students as inferior people without practical knowledge. This photograph is staged and depicts the home of a non-Native host family participating in the Sherman Outing Program. The older female or host is shown familiarizing a Sherman student to the family's electrical vacuum. The photographer may have intended to depict paternalism, but the artist wanted to offer an interesting photograph of a student working in a modern environment.

2.32. A major emphasis of the curriculum for women at Sherman included caring for babies and young children. Female teachers taught Sherman girls the "modern" techniques of childcare. Instructors at Sherman taught female students to babysit and tend households. These girls could further pursue employment by participating in the Outing Program. They lived with and worked for non-Indian families throughout Southern California.

2.33. To prepare Sherman girls to care for babies and young children as babysitters and maids, Sherman instructors taught students on campus to care for children. Sherman hosted its own daycare center long before the concept was popular, and employees and neighbors could drop off their children so students could learn to care for small children. In their own communities, Native American females received a great deal of experience caring for younger siblings and children from extended families. On reservations, older female students entered school with practical experience in childcare, prenatal care, and birthing. At Sherman Institute, young Native American women wore white uniforms and hats like nurses. They learned the "modern" methods of childcare, the kind of care non-Indians would expect of Sherman women working in their homes.

CHAPTER THREE

Sports

Sports played a prominent role in the life of all students at Sherman Institute. Like the other off-reservation American Indian boarding schools, boys and girls at Sherman engaged in a variety of sports. After 1879 when Congress established the first large Indian school, the Carlisle Indian Industrial School paved the way for other American Indian boarding schools to engage in sports. At Carlisle, Superintendent Richard Henry Pratt had found that high profile sports brought national and international attention to the school. Student athletes played on a national level that brought money and fame to Indian schools. Haskell, Chemawa, Flandreau, Riverside, Bacone, and other Indian schools followed Carlisle into the ranks of big league college sports. Most of the extramural sports focused attention on male sports, but some schools also featured extramural sports for females. Although Sherman became the last of the large off-reservation American Indian boarding schools, the Institute enjoyed a robust athletic tradition from the outset. In fact, before the Office of Indian Education built Sherman, students at Perris Indian School played sports, and images at the Sherman Indian Museum show boys and girls at Perris playing sports.

Students at Sherman Institute played a variety of sports, including inter-mural and extra-mural games. Sherman girls played against other girls at school, just as the boys played against other boys at Sherman. The school had a large intramural sports program, offering many opportunities for all children to engage in sports. Sherman also required both boys and girls to take physical education, believing that physical education provided students formal education in healthy activities. Often clubs and dorms at Sherman Institute played against each other, offering students many opportunities to watch their fellow students compete.

> *"Student athletes played on a national level that brought money and fame to Indian schools."*

Students held inter-mural tournaments against one another, and both boys and girls competed with each other in a variety of sports on campus. Sherman girls and boys played football, field hockey, basketball, track and field, softball, volleyball, weightlifting, boxing, and others. They also engaged in archery, bicycle riding, running, tennis, badminton, and weightlifting.

Significant to Sherman's history, from 1902 forward, students at the Indian School on Magnolia Avenue played sports against other schools, including high schools and colleges. Sherman teams played against other Indian schools but usually against non-Indian schools located in Southern California. Teams composed of Sherman students represented the Indian school in many sports and competed throughout the region, bringing great notoriety to the school and students. In 1900, Indian students at Perris Indian School selected the regal school colors. Two years later when the Indian Office built Sherman Institute, the students agreed to keep their school colors. Sherman students also chose the Braves as their mascot, and contemporary students proudly use this mascot today.

In their colorful uniforms, student athletes at Sherman Institute competed against students from many other schools, including colleges. Sherman boys competed against other teams in football, basketball, baseball, wresting, boxing, weight lifting, swimming, and track and field. Sherman girls played field hockey, basketball, volleyball, softball, track and field, and swimming. Sherman always fielded competitive teams, and in the early twentieth century, Sherman Braves often defeated local college teams like those at the University of California, Los Angeles, and the University of Southern California. Sherman football teams had great success playing USC. During one game, the Sherman Braves were defeating the USC Trojans so badly they left the field before the game ended, the coaches saying the team needed to return to Los Angeles and did not want to miss the train. Times have changed, of course, but Sherman Institute once fielded talented young men who could compete on the college level and succeed. Even after Sherman became an accredited high school, the campus continued to support strong sports programs for girls and boys.

Sherman sports teams were part of the national plan to assimilate Indian students. Many Indian boys and girls wanted to attend Sherman Institute so they could play major sports, other than the games they had come to know in their own communities. Baseball, basketball, softball, swimming, and running had long been central sports in Indian country, and they remained significant throughout the twentieth century. Sherman offered boys and girls an opportunity to excel on a higher level, which brought attention to the school, which was a goal of school superintendents. In the eyes of reformers, sports were another method of assimilation, but to many Sherman students, sports provided an opportunity to compete and excel against non-Indian players. Even in the face of racist jeers, Sherman fielded teams of young females and males that took pride in defeating non-Indian students and demonstrating their superiority on the playing fields and ball courts. Native American students used organized sports to demonstrate their abilities in a wide range of activities. The pride of young athletes at Sherman Institute shows on the faces of the students in many of the images preserved at the school. The photographic collection at the Sherman Indian Museum is rich in shadows showing pride and pleasure at many sporting events. Only a few of these images appear herein, but they clearly illustrate the importance of sports as one element of Sherman's rich and colorful history.

•••

3.1. Women at Sherman Institute fielded strong athletic teams, which became a tradition for the school. Women had enjoyed winning teams at Perris Indian School and they brought the winning attitude to Sherman Institute. In 1904, the Sherman girls' basketball team won the league championship, and they posed for this staged photograph. The young men and women attending Sherman participated in many forms of sport. Sherman women worked hard in their athletic programs and enjoyed the fruits of their success. The young women shown in this photograph wear discreet forms of uniforms. These uniforms, most likely in purple and gold school colors, look more like summer dresses than uniforms, but Sherman women played basketball games in these outfits.

3.2. [Above] From the Indian school days at Perris Indian School, female students competed widely in basketball. In 1938, the girls' basketball team at Sherman Institute included, from left to right, Ms. J. Chavez, V. White, G. Hillman, Coach Perkinson, P. Hicks, E. Williams, and H. McNeal. Note the change in uniforms between the 1923 and the 1938 teams. Women's basketball remains a significant sport at Sherman Indian High School.

3.3. [Below] Photographers at Sherman sometimes took candid shots of classes at the school. People with cameras sometimes slipped into a course to capture pictures that were not staged. This photograph caught the tip-off at a girls' basketball game in the gymnasium at Sherman Institute. This photograph depicts a girls Physical Education class.

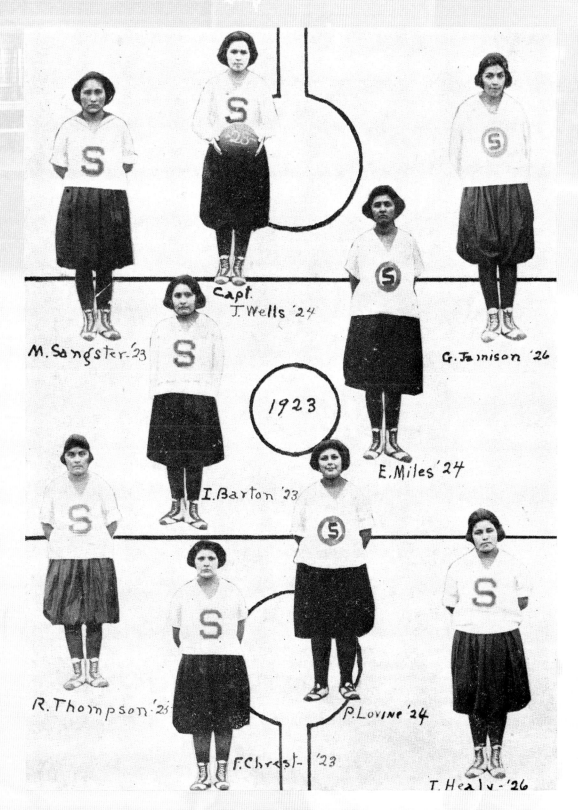

3.4. This photograph is from the Sherman Annual, which was also called The Purple and Gold. It portrays the women's basketball team at Sherman Institute in 1923. Although written in small letters, the photograph identifies the last name of each player, including team captain J. Wells, M. Sangster, G. Jamison, I. Barton, E. Mile, R. Thompson, F. Chrest, P. Lovine, and T. Healy.

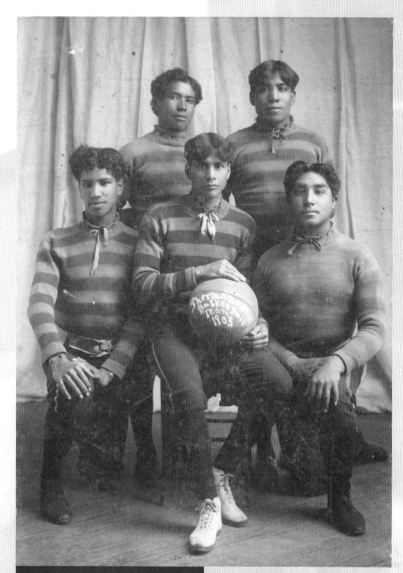

3.5. [Left] Basketball was a major sport on many reservations and played by Native American boys and girls in schools throughout the United States. In 1903, the male basketball team at Sherman Institute won a championship of their division. The 1903 championship boys' basketball team at Sherman included, from left to right, George Magee, Alex Tortes, Alex Magee, John Pugh, and John Ward. Notice the stripped uniforms with the school colors of Purple and Gold.

3.6. [Below] Sherman Institute boasted a sizable gymnasium with a maple wood floor. Sherman men and women's teams hosted numerous schools in basketball competitions. Both women's and men's basketball were extremely popular at Sherman. In fact, basketball found a huge number of fans on Indian reservations throughout the United States. Note the Sherman players are in the light colored "home" jerseys with the team name "Braves" across their chest.

3.7. According to Sherman historian Galen Townsend, students, the general public, and the White Mountain Apache Tribe considered José Coyote, a star basketball player. During his day, Coyote was "the Kareem Abdul Jabar of his day in this region of the country." The photograph shows some of the basketball team who played for Sherman Institute. In 1926, with Coyote at the helm, the Sherman Boys' Basketball team won several championships. Sherman's sports teams played both Native and non-Native schools. Note the inscription reads: "From Jose Coyote To Mr. Cells."

3.8. Six members of the Sherman boys' basketball team pose outside the old gymnasium. Although the photograph was taken in black and white, given the technology of the time, the boys' sported uniforms of golden yellow and deep purple. In 1902, students at Sherman Institute decided to keep the school colors the Indian students at the Perris Indian School had chosen in the 1890s, the royal colors of Purple and God.

3.9. Each year, photographers assigned to Sherman Institute took candid and staged group shots of the various athletic teams. This photograph depicts the Sherman boys' basketball team, complete with one team member holding a basketball and another holding a small dog, the teams unofficial mascot. The students are from the Junior High School classes at Sherman. According to Sherman historian Galen Townsend, several teams at Sherman adopted a stray dog as their mascot, which some team members believed brought them good luck.

3.10. School officials opened the doors of the school to students in 1902. In the same year, Superintendent Harwood Hall established the Sherman football team. Many of the young men that played football in 1904 had played for the Perris Indian School. Some of the football players were older than other high school students. Some of the young men were of college age, but because they had received so little formal education, they attended Sherman Institute. From the very start of the school, Sherman students built successful athletic programs, and the football teams proved to be stellar from the outset. The football teams competed with local colleges and universities. Note the young player in the middle of the picture with an open leather helmet that appears more like ear guards than a full helmet.

3.11. In the photographic collection at Sherman Indian Museum, several images exist depicting athletic teams. In addition, a few photographs exist of individuals who participated in one sport or another but especially football. During the school year, photographers took images of individual athletes. Some of these individual photographs appear in the Sherman school annuals. A few of the photographs can be found in the photographic collection. This photograph depicts a sophomore athlete named Byron Webb in 1941. Webb was a football player who played left end for the Sherman Braves. Note that the back of Webb's helmet seems to include a feather.

3.12. Football was a major sport at all the off-reservation American Indian boarding schools in the United States. Carlisle Superintendent Richard Henry Pratt used football and other sports to capture national attention and bring positive publicity to his boarding school. Sports of all kinds existed at the Perris Indian School. When Superintendent Harwood Hall moved the Indian school to Riverside, he fully promoted football. He claimed the sport encouraged good health and served as one form of assimilation into the dominant society. Football also brought funds and notoriety to Sherman and other off-reservation boarding schools. This is one of many photographs of the Sherman football team in the early twentieth century. Sherman football proved to be a dominant force in Southern California.

3.13. Every year, photographers took pictures of Sherman's teams, but not all of them have survived. Those images that still exist are found in the collection of the Sherman Indian Museum. Fortunately, the photograph of the 1908 Sherman football team still exists. Football was the most popular sport at Sherman Institute, as students always considered it a source of pride every time they beat local colleges in the early twentieth century, like the University of Southern California. Note that the players wear different uniforms that do not match.

3.14. Native Americans are known historically to be great runners, particularly long-distance runners. On many reservations, Native Americans had a tradition of running. Hopi Indians ran up and down the mesas near their homes in Northern Arizona, while Chemehuevi runners trekked across the Mojave and Colorado Deserts. Some Chemehuevi claim that their special class of runners could teleport. The traditions of Indian running came to Sherman in the form of young, talented runners who competed on local, national, and international stages. In this photograph, six Sherman runners are photographed as members of the Sherman track and field team.

3.15. "On your mark; get set; go!" Native American men and women excelled in many sports, including track and field. In this photograph, three American Indian athletes took their stance to run the one hundred yard dash. Sherman was known for its great Indian runners and award winning track teams. This photograph was taken on the Sherman track and field located on the main campus in Riverside.

3.16. [Left] Women competed in many types of track and field events at Sherman Institute. This student takes her turn in a high jump competition on the Sherman campus. During the spring, Sherman hosted many track and field meets. Students and members of the Riverside community often attended track meets to watch the competition. In an age before Title IX mandated equal funding and opportunities for both males and females in sports, Sherman offered an impressive number of competitive sports for female students.

3.17. [Below] At Sherman Institute, both boys and girls competed in intramural and extramural sports. This photograph depicts two women competing in a low hurdle race before a crowd of onlookers on the Sherman campus. Sporting events were always popular at Sherman and well supported by the student body. Athletics was a source of pride at Sherman Institute.

3.18. [Above] Sherman students called themselves the Braves in honor of Native American warriors. Athletes, dancers, and band members proudly wore the Purple and Gold. This candid photograph provides an image of baton twirlers at Sherman Institute sporting headbands, concho belts, and cowboy boots. The lead twirler wore a Plains Indian-style headdress, one not Native to California but associated with Comanche, Lakota, Dakota, Kiowa, Ponca, and other indigenous people of the Great Plains.

3.19. [Below] Young women at Sherman Institute joined many clubs. Some of the clubs only allowed women to participate. This included the Bicycle Club, which Sherman females had created. In this dramatic photograph, all these girls are holding a similar kind of bicycle. It is unclear from the records if each girl earned their bicycle or if the school or other patron bought the bicycles for these women. It appears from this photograph, the only known image of the girl's bicycle club, that the young women of Sherman enjoyed riding.

3.20. School superintendents at all the boarding schools emphasized physical education, which was part of the program to teach students to be healthy and to care for their bodies. As part of sports training and classes, coaches emphasized weight training and muscle building. Boys at Sherman Institute competed in boxing and weight lifting. Schools near and far respected the boxing and weight lifting teams at Sherman. This photograph depicts a Sherman team taken at the school. On the left is Coach Leo Haven.

3.21. During the 1890s, the public health movement emerged in the United States, especially in the urban areas of the county. Public health advocates sought to curb deaths caused by unsanitary and dangerous conditions, like isolating people known to have communicable diseases. By the time the federal government built Sherman Institute, the public health movement and knowledge about bacteria as a cause of disease and deaths was well known in the Western world. To fight disease, instructors at Sherman taught children a good deal about Public Health and germ theory, including the advantages of the use of soap. As part of the hygiene program at Sherman, boys and girls took several showers each week. This photograph depicts two Navajo boys showering, circa 1950.

CHAPTER FOUR

Music, Fine Arts, and Social Life

Music and fine arts played a significant role at Sherman Institute. Of course the Native American students at Sherman came to the Indian School on Magnolia Avenue from traditions of music, song, and fine arts. They came to Sherman with knowledge of basketry, pottery, woodcarving, jewelry making, painting, sculpture, beadwork, clothing fashion, tool making, architecture, and a host of other arts. Sherman students had seen their people make hats, shoes, intaglios, shell work, and a host of goods made from leather, bone, stone, and wood. Native American arts existed on the North American continent long before the arrival of the Vikings, Spanish, French, Dutch, Russians, or English. But most non-Indian reformers, especially those associated with the Indian Office, saw indigenous arts as "primitive" or quaint crafts, certainly not real art. They did not view Native American art forms as fine art. At Sherman, school officials provided Native American students the opportunity to learn "civilized" and accomplished forms of art. Therefore the curriculum at Sherman Institute and other off-reservation American Indian boarding schools did not reflect the rich artistic traditions of indigenous people but rather those of the newcomers. The focus of music and the arts taught at Sherman reflected that found in the dominant society. Many students gravitated to these art forms without forsaking those of their people. Some students specifically asked to enter Sherman Institute so they could study music or other fine arts. At Sherman, they learned to play musical instruments and create new forms of fine arts.

Several images found at Sherman Indian Museum illustrate the role of music and the fine arts at Sherman Institute. Native American students attending Sherman Institute represented tribes with high levels of creativity, imagination, theater, and beautiful forms of art and music. But at Sherman, they learned new forms of the fine arts that they took back to their people and shared with others. Some students remained on their reservations to teach their new art forms, but others ventured out into the larger communities of the United States where they enriched music and the fine arts. Sherman students developed their own sense of the aesthetics, and indigenous art forms have contributed to the ever-changing arts of the country.

Students at Sherman Institute had other knowledge of the fine arts based on the traditions of their people. For thousands of years, Native American historians and storytellers captured the ancient past and more recent record through strong and accurate oral traditions. They came to Sherman with detailed knowledge of oratory, theater, drama, and the medical arts. Native artistry included wonderful storytelling, songs, ritual reenactments, drama, dance, and music. Students had grown up hearing song-stories, particularly creation stories of how the people came to be and their deep connection to their sacred landscapes. A great diversity of fine art forms existed before the United States built Sherman Institute, but the Indian School on Magnolia Avenue offered its own forms of music, dance, song, and fine arts that added to traditional forms of Native art, especially music.

Students at Sherman Institute had opportunities to learn new musical instruments. In their own communities they had known of many forms of drums, rattles, clappers, flutes, and string instruments, but at Sherman Institute music teachers taught boys and girls to play trombones, trumpets, clarinets, pianos, violins, guitars, tubas, piccolos, and a host of other instruments. In addition to learning new instruments, Native American students attending Sherman could play their instruments in one of several venues. At Sherman Institute, students could join the marching band, play in an orchestra, and join small groups that performed a variety of musical styles. Many students joined smaller musical groups, using their musical talents to form their own bands to play classical, modern, country western, and jazz music.

Photographs preserved in the archives of the Sherman Indian Museum depicts students engaged in all these forms of music. In addition, images show Native American students singing in various choir groups that became famous in the area. Choral and musical groups traveled throughout Southern California and beyond, giving concerts that publicly confirmed that the assimilation program of Sherman Institute had accomplished its goals among the student population. Sherman students often played classical music, offering concerts that featured the works of Mozart, Bach, Beethoven, Shubert, Tchaikovsky, and other European masters. While the photographs depict Sherman

> *"...Sherman Institute had successfully assimilated students into the fabric of American patriotism and militarism."*

students sharing Western musical traditions, the images could not express the continuance and expansion of art forms traditional to Native American students who would not abandon their Native forms of song and music but dynamically incorporate new forms of music and other arts into their communities. In a very real sense, Sherman students "turned the power" and used their new knowledge to enrich Native American cultures and communities. Sherman students of the arts demonstrated their ability to grow and expand in innovative ways.

Not long after the government built Sherman Institute, Sherman Superintendent Harwood Hall successfully built an auditorium so students could perform music and theater in a large facility that provided a venue for students and the general public. Students performed concerts and plays in the school auditorium. Select Sherman girls organized a mandolin club, and they mastered the small string instrument that was very

4.1. Officials at Sherman Institute emphasized American nationalism and patriotism of the United States. On several holidays, the school band performed patriotic music in the school auditorium. Students at Sherman experienced flag ceremonies every day, and they learned to march by and salute the Stars and Stripes situated on the flagpole located near the entrance of campus off Magnolia Avenue. This photograph was taken in the school auditorium and depicts the Sherman Institute band seated in front of an oversized American flag and flanked by four additional American flags and a bald eagle on both sides.

popular during the early twentieth century. Members of the all-female mandolin club became highly skilled in presenting concerts using voice and mandolins. Girls in the Mandolin Club practiced every week and gave concerts in the auditorium as well as venues off campus.

Each year, students at Sherman put on plays, pageants, musicals, and a host of other performances. Some plays emphasized patriotism and glorified the arrival of Pilgrims and Puritans. Other plays involved the honoring of the American flag, placing the Stars and Stripes at the center of musical and theatrical performances. Several photographs depict themes of patriotism, demonstrating that Sherman Institute had successfully assimilated students into the fabric of American patriotism and militarism. Girls and boys learned patriotism of the United States, and as young military cadets, they learned to march in close order, carry rifles, and salute the American flag. Sherman students performed honor guard ceremonies, and they often participated in parades away from campus where they outwardly symbolized a love of their country.

In addition to participating in patriotic pageants and ceremonies, school officials encouraged students to participate in annual Christmas pageants. Some Sherman students had grown up Christian, but others had not participated in any of the Christian sects. Most students enjoyed celebrating Christmas because school officials cooperated with Christian churches to bring presents for students. By including Christmas in the annual calendar of events, school superintendents demonstrated to the general public and congressional leaders, who controlled school budgets, that Sherman students were learning the faith and that the Institution was a Christian school. Sherman officials used patriotic and Christian oriented performances, including plays and musical concerts, to assimilate students into the dominant society. Such participation by students also encouraged federal, state, and local budgetary support for the Indian School on Magnolia Avenue.

•••

4.2. The Boy Scouts of America had a strong program on the campus of Sherman Institute. The Boy Scouts taught American patriotism and all the rules associated with handling, folding, and flying the Stars and Stripes. Sherman fostered patriotism in many ways. After a ceremonial Court of Honor, the Eagle Scouts shown here received scouting's highest honor as a result of moving through the ranks and earning promotions by achieving several merit badges. At Sherman Institute, Boy Scouts participated in many activities, including cooking, leatherwork, and first aid. Native Americans never exposed to the Western world would have grown up practicing many of the skills taught to Boy Scouts. Notice in this rare photograph that these Native American Scouts displayed many merit badges onto the sashes.

4.3. [Left] The Girl Scouts of America fostered an active troop of girls at Sherman Institute. Like the Boy Scout troop at Sherman, female students learned about camping, cooking, and cleaning. They also learned different arts, including beading as seen here. Note that while school officials frowned on Native American styled beadwork at school, these Sherman girls were instructed in the beading of non-Native designs. Both Girl Scouts and Boy Scouts proved another method used by school officials to assimilate Native Americans and teach them loyalty to the United States.

4.4. [Below] Many of the off-reservation boarding schools and some of the on-reservation boarding schools sponsored their own Boy Scout and Girl Scout troops. This photograph depicts Sherman Institutes' own Boy Scout Troop 10, which was based in Riverside, California, and part of the general council of Scouts in the region. The school's Outing Program encouraged assimilation, patriotism, and practical skills. Notice the boy at the bottom left carrying a bugle, an instrument also used on the Sherman campus during flag ceremonies.

4.5. The photograph depicts four drama students and their instructor. For thousands of years and long before the federal government established Sherman Institute, Native American tribes throughout the Americas practiced many forms of drama. During a visit to a Delaware village in Pennsylvania, a Moravian missionary received a shock when a medicine man jumped into the village as if to terrorize the villagers. The Bear Doctor had been asked to treat a patient, but the Moravian believed the bear to be an animal. Selected students at Sherman took a formal course of study in drama, and students trained in the art of drama. Several students performed on stage, and student helpers instructed younger children in acting, particularly for school plays of patriotic or classical themes. Some groups even toured the United States, including the one shown here.

4.6. Shortly after the federal government got the construction of Sherman Institute underway, Superintendent Harwood Hall advocated for an augmentation to build an auditorium. He wanted to highlight the civilization process as seen through dramatic and musical performances by American Indian children. Even before Hall built the school hospital, he had the auditorium built. Sherman Institute boasted an excellent auditorium that held many people. Teachers used the facility for many productions that situated students into mainstream, non-Native America. For example, the production pictured here is of "Little Ferries" that relies exclusively on the European style of theater. Note that the teachers had two of the Indian girls presented in black face for this production. Other students appear in their daily military dress. Also note Santa Claus standing in the middle of this unique photograph and the strange, enlarged head pieces of two students.

4.7. In this ironic photograph, a Sherman boy and girl appear here dressed as Pilgrims who arrived in Massachusetts in 1620. This performance may have been for Thanksgiving. Most Native Americans knew little about colonial American history in the eastern part of the United States. They had grown up hearing songs and stories about their own people, which may have included stories about the coming of non-Indians into their countries. Some of the children that attended Sherman in the early twentieth century had heard stories about the Indian Wars in the American West, but few likely know about the settlers of Jamestown and Massachusetts Bay. This priceless photograph depicts a school play in the auditorium of Sherman Institute representing the arrival of Pilgrims in 1621. Note the Mayflower sailing into the Atlantic or great bay east of present-day Boston. Sherman often produced patriotic plays depicting significant topics in American history, which was one way of teaching school children the history of the United States and promoting patriotism.

4.8. [Above] In front of a giant American flag, Sherman boys and girls appear dressed in colonial attire and sing patriotic songs. Students celebrated the English landing in New England. They did not celebrate their Native roots or the place of indigenous people in American history, one of many ironies found at the off-reservation boarding school. Note the two figures elevated in the center appear to be George and Martha Washington. Fortunately, today talented teachers instruct Sherman students about American Indian history, language, and culture.

4.9. [Below] Students attending Sherman Institute came from tribes with deep traditions in song and music. Native Americans played flutes, drums, rattles, clappers, and a host of instruments not common to the people of the West. Many students attended American Indian boarding schools so they could learn musical instruments brought to the Americas by European settlers. Several Sherman girls learned to play the mandolin, a small, 8-string instrument that originated in the eighth century. Female students formed a musical group centered on the playing of the mandolin, a member of the flute family. Young women interested in the instrument worked extra hard to be part of a musical group known as the Mandolin Club, and they performed on campus and at different venues around Southern California.

4.10. The Sherman curriculum included classical music, and superintendents enjoyed having the Indian students perform classical on campus and in the cities of Southern California. Sherman girls and boys played musical instruments and contributed to the many forms of music known at the school. For school officials, classical concerts represented another outward verification that Sherman was fulfilling its mission of assimilating Native American youth into civilized America. This photograph from the collection at Sherman Indian Museum shows students at a concert. A photographer posed the students on the stage of Sherman's auditorium before a formal performance to take the image presented here. The Sherman music program fostered the musicality of native students in the western style of classical music.

4.11. The Sherman marching band played the school fight song at football games and other athletic events. In this photograph, only boys appear, perhaps because this is a military band. But Sherman girls also participated in the bands as well. The Sherman marching band also performed in parades held throughout Southern California, including the Rose Parade in Pasadena, California. The Sherman marching band wore the Purple and Gold during their performances in downtown Riverside, California, where they played for the guests of Frank Miller's Mission Inn Hotel.

4.12. [Above] During the 1940s, a new and exciting style of music emerged. Many related this era to the music of the day, commonly calling it the Big Band Era. A new form of dance emerged with the Big Bands, especially Swing, which made the young people "jive" to the tunes of Count Basie, Buddy Rich, Glen Miller, Ray Anthony, Cab Calloway, Dorsey Brothers, Gene Krupa, Benny Goodman, Louis Armstrong, and Big Bad Voodoo Daddy. This was the music of World War II, and talented students at Sherman played the music to the delight of others. Pictured here in the front row, left to right, include Max Mazetti (Rincon) and in the back, upper right, Robert Levi (Torres Martinez). In the front right is the Band Director, Patrick Miguel (Quechan/ Fort Yuma). Notice that all the band members are males but a female accompanies them on the piano.

4.13. [Below] As the years passed during the twentieth century, school officials became more lenient about the kinds of music student could perform on campus. As a result, students enjoyed rock and roll, jazz, classical, and country-western. During the 1960s, five Sherman boys formed a Country-Western band called The Country Polka, and these young men played tunes by Sonny James, Roy Clark, Patsy Cline, Chet Atkins, Buck Owens, Tammy Wynette, Loretta Lynn, and other popular country stars. They also shared their own original songs when they played at school dances, concerts, and other social events. Note that the band includes three electric guitars, amp, and acoustical guitar.

4.14. A Sherman girl poses for a photograph in her tribe's traditional dress. To confound the viewer, this young Sherman woman plays her violin, which she had learned to play at Sherman, while taking and preserving pride in her Native heritage. Although music teachers had taught her to play a violin, a non-Native musical instrument, this student never forgot their Native heritage. She portrays the paradox: A "primitive" Indian in Native dress with the sophisticated ability to play violin. Clearly, the image tries to convey, this Sherman woman has been influenced successfully by assimilation at the Indian School on Magnolia Avenue.

4.15. Teachers at Sherman encouraged students to branch out and explore many types of music and instruments, including Big Band, Bluegrass, Dixieland, and Country. Music instructors also introduced young Sherman students to new instruments, including the banjo. Originally created in American by African Americans, the instrument emerged from an African instrument of similar design. African American musicians mastered and built the first banjos, which became popular throughout the United States. The banjo generally has four strings, as in this photograph, but sometimes banjos have five strings. Both kinds of banjos produce a distinct sound. One of the Sherman students learned to play the banjo and shared his talents with members of the student body.

4.16. Although administrators at Sherman Institute professed to seek the assimilation of American Indian students, school officials allowed—and sometimes, encouraged—Native American students to don their traditional clothing. In 1926, Martin Felix Napa posed for this photograph in traditional Navajo clothing, although he wears a headdress not used by his people but those of the Great Plains. At Sherman Institute and while in college in Oklahoma, Napa was known for his excellent voice, often entertaining others by singing "Old Man River." During World War II, Napa served as a Marine and Navajo Code Talker. He was badly wounded while scouting behind Japanese lines and he died on May 1, 1965, while marching in a VFW Loyalty Day Parade in Gallup, New Mexico. Napa was one of many American Indian veterans that had attended the Indian School on Magnolia Avenue.

4.17. [Above] In comparison to traditional dress of Native Americans, school officials issued military uniforms that Sherman students had to wear. In the early twentieth century, Sherman boys and girls wore military style uniforms, just like Native American students at Carlisle, Haskell, Chemawa, Riverside, and other American Indian boarding schools. The military uniforms looked like the one depicted in this photograph. All Sherman students experienced military drill and rigor. School officials used a military model first established at Carlisle Indian Industrial School where Captain Richard Henry Pratt sought to "break" the pattern of indigenous cultural ways and essentially "kill the Indian and save the man." Sherman students learned the military ways of the United States at Sherman and went on to serve with distinction in the armed forces. The Sherman cadet in this photograph wears a smart uniform, carries a sword, and has earned three medals.

4.18. [Right] John Nick, a Navajo student, sat for his portrait at Sherman Institute. Only a few of the photographs found in the collection of the Sherman Indian Museum depict students dressed in Native clothing. In this special photograph, Sherman student John Nick posed for his portrait wearing a Plains Indian headdress and Pendleton blanket. Navajo people had their own form of headdress, but not that of Plains Indians. However, Plains Indian headdresses spoke to non-Native people that attended performances and witnessed John Nick's performances. This handsome young man inscribed this photograph, which reads: "yours truly John Nick class of 1926."

Yours truly
John Nick
Class of 1926

4.19. Until the 1930s and the administration of President Franklin D. Roosevelt, Sherman students rarely performed traditional dances and song. When they did, superintendents controlled the venues. This changed after the 1930s when superintendents allowed students greater freedom to conduct indigenous dance, song, and music. Native Americans of the Southwest and Great Plains performed variations of the Hoop Dance and Eagle Dance. In this photograph, Sherman students, most likely from one of the Great Plains tribes, pose before dancing and drumming. The boy on the left performed the Eagle Dance and the boy on the right did the Hoop Dance. Note the boys wear eagle feathers, bells, moccasins, beadwork items, and thin bone chest plates. Since the Indian New Deal of the Great Depression era, some Sherman students have celebrated selected aspects of Native American song, dance, and drumming with various performances. In addition, after World War II, Sherman Institute began hosting an annual Pow Wow, which continues today.

4.20. On many reservations, Native Americans decorated their horses for parades, war, and ceremony. For special occasions, American Indians painted their horse and placed ribbons, feathers, and beaded masks on their horses. With the coming of automobiles and trucks, some Native Americans decorated their vehicles to celebrate important events or ceremonies. During the 1960s, Sherman students from many backgrounds decorated their vehicles for a parade. This photograph depicts a car with a tipi decoration made in celebration of Sherman Day. Students from the Hualapai and Havasupai tribes placed this makeshift tipi on the back of a small Ford convertible. Neither the Hualapai nor Havasupai of Arizona used tipis as their homes. These high school students likely used the tipi motif as a tongue-in-cheek joke or gesture of humor that Native Americans would understand.

4.21. From the beginning of Sherman Institute, superintendents and teachers liked students to perform plays. In 1946, the Office of Indian Education created the Five Year Navajo Program that admitted only Navajo students to Sherman Institute. During the 1950s, Sherman Institute used several Navajo examples within the curriculum so that the school would relate better to the tribal students. The photograph depicts one example of inclusion of Navajo themes at Sherman. The students in this image present a dramatic play in the school auditorium that included elements of Navajo culture, including dresses, headbands, silver jewelry, woven rug, and female hogan (Navajo home). Students reenact elements of their traditional culture, performing a play based on life in Dinetah, homeland of Navajo people.

4.22. As part of the assimilation process, school officials encouraged Native American students to form clubs and be a part of the larger school scene. Like many elements of the boarding school experience, tribal students used the clubs to strengthen the bond between each other, especially after World War II when superintendents and teachers were less interested in destroying Native American culture. The Apache-Yavapai Club included students that had learned Mountain Spirit songs and dances. Men and women participating in the Apache-Yavapai Club established a dance team to perform on and off campus. The students made their own outfits, often with the help of their parents and grandparents, and they learned the dramatic songs and dances associated with the gaans or Mountain Spirits. The dances they performed had deep meaning, in part depicting the spiritual conflict between positive and negative forces. Girls and boys participated in Mountain Spirit Dances. Males and females learned the songs, dance sequences, and drumming. On the far left, the Apache clown was painted with spots on his body; he carried a bullroarer. The students used a water drum to create music. Two girls wear beaded chokers, and some of the students wear high-top moccasins. Note the ornately painted wooden headdresses made of yucca stems worn by some of the male dancers, but not the clown.

4.23. In this photograph, six Sherman girls pose with their dorm advisor during a Christmas party complete with Santa Claus. Rather than return home for the holidays, Sherman girls and boys generally remained on campus to celebrate the season with their "Sherman Family." Administrators wanted Sherman students to celebrate Christmas and other Christian holidays as part of the effort to assimilate Native students. However, some American Indian families had celebrated Christmas long before the government built the Indian School on Magnolia Avenue.

4.24. As part of the assimilation program at Sherman Institute, school officials encouraged students to participate in the holidays celebrated by the dominant society. American Indian students celebrated Easter, Flag Day, and July 4. Sherman students honored Armistice Day in early November and Thanksgiving later that same month. In this photograph, Native American girls gathered around the Christmas tree in their dorm to open presents on Christmas morning. The school and churches bought gifts for Sherman children, at times bringing them stockings full of fruit, nuts, and candy. Students celebrated Christmas by singing carols and performing Christmas pageants.

4.25. This photograph depicts seven shepherds with crooked staffs and three angels. Each year, students celebrated the Christian holiday of Christmas. Students gave each other and teachers cards and gifts. They sang Christmas carols and sometimes sang carols, traveling from dorm to dorm. Sherman students also performed a Christmas pageant that had deep roots in the Christian religion. This photograph depicts a reenactment of the Biblical story of Jesus' birth. The students performed the Christmas story in the school auditorium. This photograph demonstrates a common activity at Sherman Institute with students representing the angel that appeared to the shepherds in the hills near Bethlehem. School superintendents suppressed Native American religions but they supported Christian celebrations. Catholic and Protestant churches and Christian organizations brought gifts and clothing to Sherman students as part of their outreach to students.

4.26. As part of the Christmas celebration at Sherman, drama and music teachers planned and executed a Nativity play, which students shared with each other and the general public. This photograph shows Sherman students performing a nativity play, depicting the birth of Jesus on the first Christmas. The play included Mary, Joseph, shepherds, wise men, and a manger for baby Jesus. Ester Damon, a Navajo student from the notable Navajo family, played Mary in this play production. Christianity played an important role in the assimilation program at Sherman, and students often remembered this time of year in a positive way. At Christmas time, students ate delicious food and received treats from the school and churches. Most students also celebrated Christmas at the church they attended throughout the year.

4.27. This photograph provides a unique image of four boys and one girl playing pool or pocket billiards. The pool table offered one form of recreation for Sherman students and another site where boys and girls could interact with each other without oppressive monitoring of Sherman officials. A pool table at Sherman Institute appears contradictory to the school's aim of clean living and positive values. In the early twentieth century, many people considered pool halls dens of iniquity and negative influences on young people. Yet, shooting pool offered another form of recreation at the school and likely encouraged young people to remain on campus to play billiards and not venture to local pool halls.

CHAPTER FIVE

Religion and Health

Separation of church and state was one of the fundamental principles guiding the Founding Fathers in the formation of the United States. Thomas Jefferson particularly championed the separation of church and state in order to further the concepts of freedom of religion within the new nation and to keep religious leaders from influencing the government from within. However, over the course of American history, different branches of government and many governmental officials ignored the separation of church and state to champion Christianity, especially Protestantism, as the one true religion of the United States. After the Civil War and the rise of the so-called "Peace Policy," the Office of Indian Affairs preferred to hire Christian missionaries as Indian superintendents and agents on reservations. Indian superintendents championed the establishment of Christian churches on reservations as part of the so-called Peace Policy. In the American Southwest and in California, many indigenous people grew up in the Catholic church and had a good deal of experience participating in the religion at the time of their matriculation into Sherman Institute. Sherman officials preferred Protestant religions but agreed to send Catholic Indians to the church built across Magnolia from Sherman.

Until 1924, most American Indians were not considered citizens of the United States and had virtually no say in national or state politics. Even after passage of the American Indian Citizenship Act, many Indians could not register to vote in state or federal elections. They did not enjoy freedom of religion and had little influence on policies at boarding schools, including Sherman. In fact, against the Jeffersonian principles of the separation of church and state, the Indian Office outlawed Native American religious practices, ceremonies, rituals, dances, and spiritual practices. In spite of national policies that discriminated against American Indian spiritual beliefs, indigenous people continued to practice their religions in private, carefully concealing ceremonies, songs, and rites to avoid conflicts with Indian police officers or soldiers.

Isolating American Indian children at off-reservation boarding schools provided Christian reformers an opportunity to break their link with traditional Native religions and bring them to Christianity. At Sherman and other off-reservation boarding schools, administrators forced Native American children to attend church services, Sunday school, and Christian group meetings. School officials punished Native American children for refusing to attend Christian functions, and they prevented students from practicing their Native religions. School officials punished children for singing traditional songs, singing or saying their prayers, conducting rituals, or participating in ceremony. No freedom of religion existed at Sherman Institute or any of the other federal boarding schools. In spite of these pointed efforts to assimilate and Christianize students, many Native American students held onto their traditional spiritual beliefs. Sherman students had to participate in Christian churches, youth organizations, and ceremonies, and they made the best of the situation. But many also held onto their own beliefs and kept their religions alive. Traditional beliefs of Sherman students remained personal in spite of assimilation promoted by teachers, counselors, and administrators at the school. For many students, their religions, cultures, and languages were sacred. Many students never forgot their ancient practices and beliefs. Other students lost elements of their cultural traditions. Without the teachings of tribal elders, who were not at the school to train students in cultural ways, some students lost their cultural ways. Some students returned to their homelands to renew their tribal traditions and help them keep them alive. Each student followed an individual path. Their worlds had been turned upside down by assimilation forced upon them by the federal government at boarding school.

Photographs found in the Sherman Indian Museum contain numerous illustrations of church activities at or near the school. Few depict Indians participating in their traditional spiritual ways until the late twentieth century, primarily in the 1960s and 1970s. Several images exist showing Sherman students attending the Protestant and Catholic churches built near campus to provide Christian instructions. Sherman students were captive audiences for Christian churches, and the various faiths influenced the course of Sherman's history by the mere presence of churches of different denominations built near Sherman Institute. Some of these churches remain close to the campus today and serve students at Sherman Indian High School. During the course of the twentieth century, other faiths established churches near Sherman and encouraged school children to attend their services.

> *"Traditional beliefs of Sherman students remained personal in spite of assimilation...."*

Some Native American children attending Sherman had grown up on reservations going to church and had been baptized into a Christian religion. They made the transition into the church services offered near Sherman without difficulty, but others had trouble adjusting. Former students often explained that they attended one service over the other because of more generous and delicious snacks or the opportunity to win prizes by memorizing Bible versus. Sometimes students attended church services as a means to pray for other students who were ill or dying at Sherman. Although Sherman boasted its own hospital, a subject well illustrated in the photographic collection, some students came to Sherman already infected with disease or contracted disease once on campus. Several photographs depict the hospital at Sherman as well as student illnesses and nurses tending patients. Some illustrations also offer different views of the school cemetery, which school officials situated south of the Sherman farm off Indiana Avenue just north of the Gage Canal.

The Sherman Bulletin

Published weekly as a regular part of the school work of Sherman Institute

Volume XVIII   Riverside, California, Feb 27, 1925.   Number 23

SHERMAN INSTITUTE PROTESTANT CHAPEL DEDICATED

The new chapel located just across the avenue from the school, a magnificent and unique building of Spanish architecture costing $32,000, was dedicated at two services Sunday, February 22, (Washington's Birthday) to the unity of Protestant services for the Indian boys and girls who shall attend this institution in future years.

The morning service which was principally for students and employees was attended by about 600 students. The afternoon service was for the white friends of the institution and was attended by about 900 people. At the morning services, Dr. George F. Kengott, superintendent of the Southern California Conference of the Congregational Church delivered the address on the subject of "Love, Education and Christian Fellowship." It was an enthusistic and inspiring

(Continued on page 3)

5.1. [Left] The Sherman Bulletin was the official voice of Sherman Institute. In this photograph, the newspaper of February 27, 1925 announced, "Sherman Institute Protestant Chapel Dedicated." Built in the Spanish Mission Revival architectural style, the Protestant Chapel cost $32,000. From 1902 forward, Sherman administrators forced students to attend either the Protestant or Catholic churches. The newspaper recorded many activities at Sherman, and school administrators reported that students wrote all the entries found in the school newspaper. This is doubtful. Still, the school newspaper provided a wealth of information.

5.2. [Above] Administrators at Sherman encouraged, and often forced, children to attend church, including the St. Thomas Catholic Church. The Catholic Diocese built St. Thomas in 1903 to provide services for Catholic students at Sherman. The church entrance faces Magnolia Avenue. This photograph depicts Sherman Catholic students, girls dressed in white dresses and hats of lace and flowers. Catholic priests sometimes wrote the Sherman school superintendent to remind him that Catholic students should attend St. Thomas and not the Protestant Chapel. Christianity was much a part of the federal Indian boarding schools, and school officials insisted that students attend one of the local churches.

5.3. In 1903, the Catholic Diocese built St. Thomas Catholic Church in the Mission Revival style, the same style used in the construction of Sherman Institute. One year after the federal government opened the doors to Sherman, the Catholic Church bought land just north of campus and built St. Thomas. The architecture of the church carried the message that it was part of the Sherman Institute, located just across the street from the Indian school.

5.4. In addition to the Catholic and Protestant churches, other denominations established buildings near Sherman Institute for the convenience of student members of those denominations. The Church of Jesus Christ of Later Day Saints, for example, built a temple on Jackson Avenue, located on the west side of the Sherman campus. The Mormon temple opened its doors to the students of Sherman Institute and local residents of the Arlington area of Riverside, California. Students were free to worship many forms of religion but they could not worship through the Sweat Lodge, pipe ceremony, or Native American Church. Students of Sherman Institute had no freedom of religion and they could not participate openly in Native American ceremonies, which some school officials and teachers considered heathenistic and primitive.

5.5. Many Native American students at Sherman grew into adulthood at school. Some fell in love. At Sherman, students met members of the opposite sex and different tribal people attending Sherman. Sometimes, students dated each other throughout school and ultimately married after their boarding school days. This photograph depicts a Catholic couple marrying at the St. Thomas Church on Magnolia Avenue. The off-reservation boarding school brought diverse tribal people together, and many "mixed" marriages took place. For example, Robert Levi was a Cahuilla Indian from the Torres Martinez Reservation. He fell in love with Ester Damon, a beautiful Navajo student at Sherman. Robert and Ester married and produced a delightful and talented family that remains in the region today.

5.6. This photograph from the archives of Sherman Indian Museum depicts a student couple that decided to be married. Rather then return to their homes for the celebration, the couple married at the Protestant Chapel at Sherman. They married at Sherman so they could invite their classmates to the wedding. Many couples that met at Sherman ultimately got married, and some of the tribal elders today in Riverside, California, met, married, and remained in Riverside, California. During the 1990s and early 2000s, the Gold Eagles of Sherman met once a month in Bennett Hall on the Sherman campus for fun and fellowship. Each month, they celebrated a reunion. Several of the couples that attended these gatherings were Sherman alums that married after their boarding school days.

5.7. Sherman students stand for a formal photograph either at a school prom or at a wedding. These young people pose with their friends. At Sherman, students sometimes held special dances and dressed in formal attire. At school dances, young men and women looked their best. The photographer captured the joy on the faces of these young people. At school dances after World War II, students danced to modern music of their eras. Notice the decorations and the clothing worn by the students.

5.8. Two students at Sherman Institute use their culinary skills to prepare for a Halloween party. They were students in a Home Economics course that trained girls to prepare meals for families or small groups. They pose in a kitchen at Sherman, a classroom setting where teachers have placed enticing signs on the wall. On the right, they placed the sign, "For Waffles" and to the left they placed the sign, "In Cake." The girl on the right churns a crank to make ice cream for other students attending the Halloween gathering.

5.9. [Bottom Left] The Sherman Hospital was one of the most important buildings on campus. It served the student population and larger Native American community of Southern California. Built in 1905, school officials at Sherman Institute completed the school hospital because of the illnesses and accidents suffered by the student body. Superintendent Harwood Hall had the hospital built in the popular mission revival style. The hospital was two stories high and offered sleeping porches for patients who slept out of doors each night. Many local Indians used the Sherman Hospital, and Field Nurses brought children to Sherman to have X-rays taken or to test them for trachoma.

5.10. [Right] When Sherman opened its doors to the first cohort up from the Perris Indian School, Superintendent Harwood Hall hired Dr. Mary Israel, a medical doctor trained in England. Because of credentialing issues, Dr. Israel hired on as an instructor of Nursing. She built a highly sophisticated Nursing Program at Sherman and trained only the best and brightest young women attending the boarding school. This photograph depicts a select group of Native American students who learned nursing through classroom lessons and practical work in the Sherman Hospital. The woman seated was their instructor.

Hospital

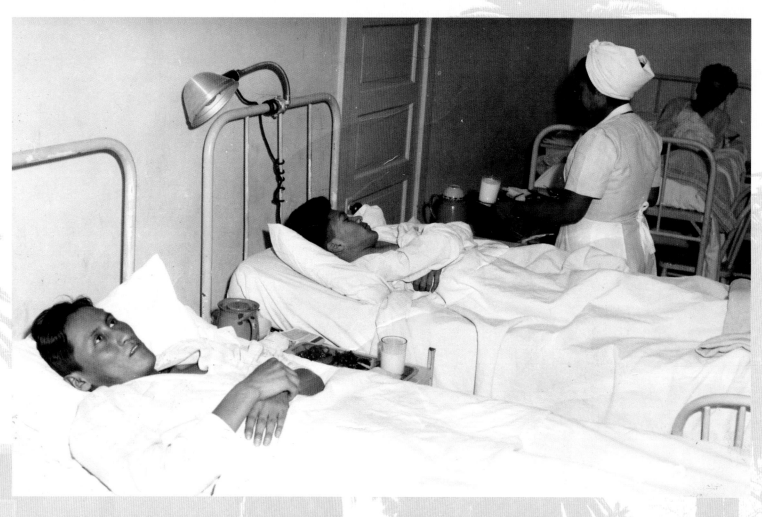

5.11. After Superintendent Hall had the Sherman Hospital built, he charged Dr. Mary Israel with the added duty of running the hospital. Although the school contracted with medical doctors to help with serious cases, Dr. Israel and the student nurses ran the hospital seven days a week and twenty-four hours each day. This photograph depicts Native American nursing students tending other students at the Sherman Hospital. Notice that the three boys in bed are very ill. The boy in the foreground has no interest in eating his lunch or drinking milk.

5.12. In 1895, German physicist Wilhelm Conrad Rontgen discovered X-Rays. In 1901, he won the Nobel Prize in Physics for his important discovery that allowed the medical profession to see inside the human body. X-rays allow doctors, nurses, and technicians to diagnose disease and broken bones. Native Americans had little access to X-rays during the early years of the twentieth century, but once the Riverside Hospital bought an X-ray machine, doctors and nurses serving the Sherman student population could use X-rays to diagnose tuberculosis, a deadly upper respiratory disease that could attack an organ or part of the body. This photograph, c. 1950, depicts a mobile X-ray unit at Sherman Institute taking pictures of lungs in search of tuberculosis or other respiratory diseases. Note the mobile TB unit with the sign, "Get Your Free X-ray, Check Your Chest, Don't Delay." Also on the mobile TB unit, is a sign with Santa, "Fight Tuberculosis, Give." Finally note the sign for the American Lung Association.

Betty Jane Begay - grad
nurses' aid in the Comm

½ Hour

1952 - working as a
pital, Riverside, Calif.

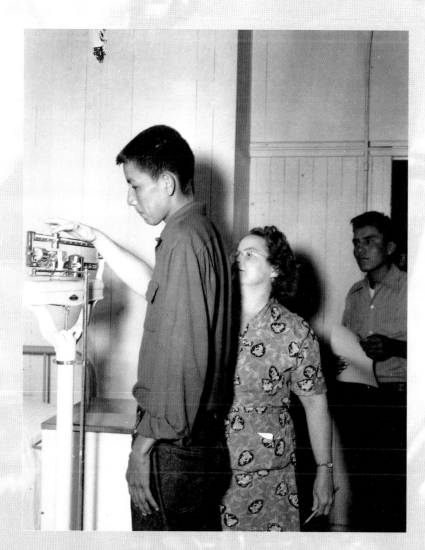

5.13. [Left] The Nursing Program at Sherman Institute trained young women to serve fellow students at the campus hospital. When Sherman nurses graduated, the Office of Indian Affairs projected that the young women would return home to serve their people or work in a hospital in towns and cities near their reservations. While at Sherman, student nurses received practical training in nursing at the school hospital and Riverside Community Hospital, a major institution in Riverside, California. This photograph from 1961, during the Navajo Program, shows Navajo student Betty Jane Begay doing an internship at Riverside Community Hospital as a nurse's aide.

5.14. [Above] This photograph represents a nurse weighing a Sherman student, recording his weight to watch for a suspicious fall in weight, a sign of tuberculosis. In 1882, German medical doctor and pioneer in microbiology, Robert Koch, published a paper on the causation of tuberculosis, showing the world that the dreadful disease stemmed from Mycobacterium tuberculosis. He proved that bacteria, not heredity, caused tuberculosis. Koch founded the field of bacteriology, and he identified the pathogens that caused cholera, anthrax, and tuberculosis. His discoveries significantly affected the history of Native Americans and students at Sherman Institute. By 1902 when Sherman opened, school officials knew about germ theory and taught elements of public health in its curriculum. In addition, they attempted to prevent tuberculosis and its spread at Sherman by recording the weight of each student to track weight loss, one sign of infection by the tuberculosis bacteria.

5.15. [Above] Nursing students at Sherman spent part of their time in the classroom listening to lectures and learning from demonstrations. They also spent hours with nursing instructors in the Sherman Hospital observing ill or injured students. In addition, when student nurses qualified, the administration assigned them duty to care for students in the school hospital. In this photograph, two female students at Sherman Institute care for a hospitalized younger student. Nursing students staffed the school hospital and received no pay for their work, although some earned Sherman Scrip.

5.16. [Below] Childcare developed into one of the main courses of study for female students at Sherman. American Indian girls and young women took classes in Home Economics that required them to learn how to care for babies and young children. Female students at Sherman Institute also received first-hand experience caring for non-Indian children in this class on campus. This photograph depicts the childcare center at Sherman where Sherman girls cared for the children of the staff, faculty, and administration. Note the slide and high bar, part of the playground equipment.

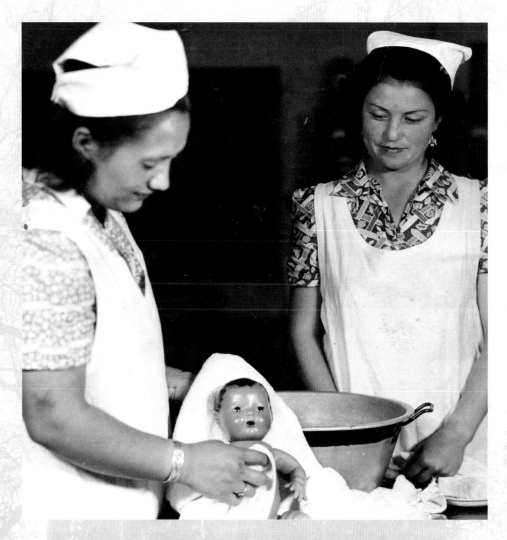

5.17. Several elements of the curriculum at Sherman emphasized childcare. Female students in the Domestic Sciences and Nursing Program spent a great deal of time learning to care for mothers and babies. This photograph illustrates a Sherman girl bathing baby dolls as a precursor to bathing babies. Another student looks on. Students in the Nursing Program at Sherman learned care for mothers and babies during the pre-natal and post-natal stages, and some nurses continued on to become "birthing doctors" or mid-wives on reservations where they employed Native American knowledge and Western knowledge.

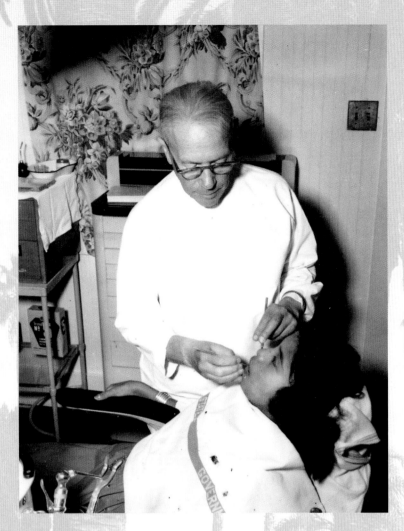

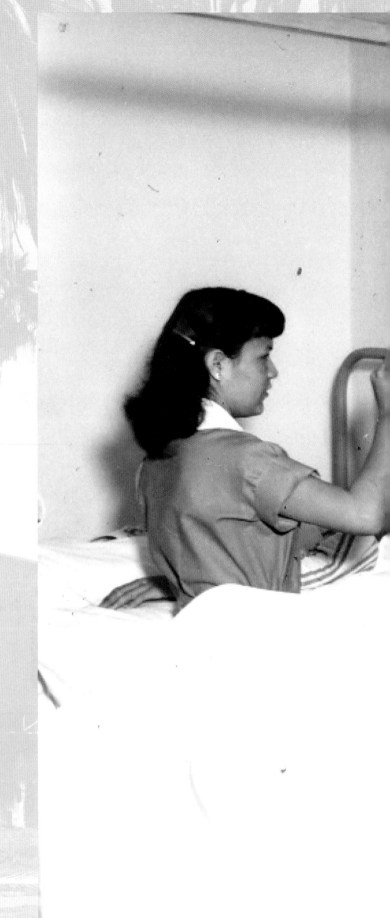

5.18. [Above] Neither Sherman Institute nor the Mission Indian Agency of Southern California hired a full time dentist to serve students or the American Indian population of the region. The Medical Division of the Bureau of Indian Affairs contracted with dentists to offer temporary service to Native Americans on and off the Sherman campus. In Riverside, California, Sherman contracted with Dr. Marcus, a specialist in dentistry, to care for the teeth of Sherman students. Here Dr. Marcus examines one of the Sherman girls.

5.19. [Right] Two young student nurses tend to two boys that officials have admitted to the Sherman Hospital. For many years, Sherman supported a sophisticated Nursing Program. Part of the school curriculum required young Sherman women to intern at the school hospital where they cared for patients with a variety of ailments, some quite serious. Because Sherman Institute was an agricultural and mechanical school that supported extramural and intramural sports, as well as classes in physical education, several students were injured while attending the boarding school. When students became injured or fell ill from disease, school administrators admitted them to the Sherman Hospital where nurses like the two in this picture oversaw the care of fellow students.

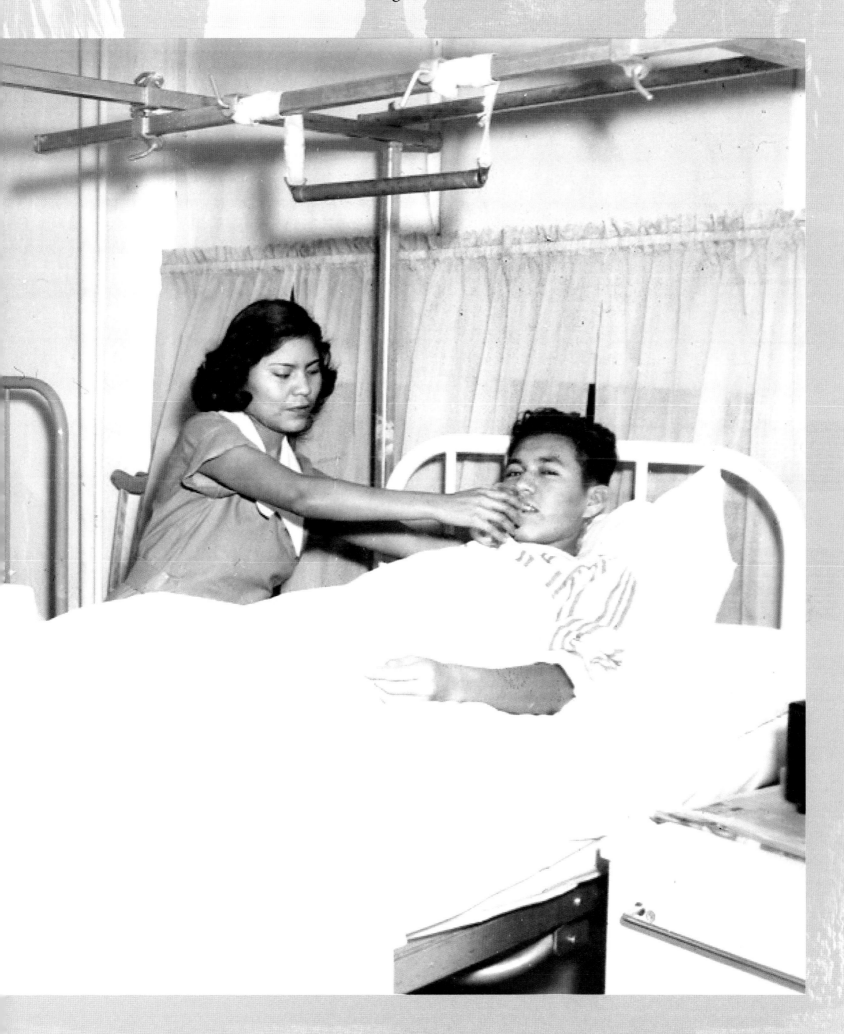

5.20. Frank Clark became one of the most notable students that ever attended Sherman Institute. This handsome young man posed for his class picture in 1940 when he was the Student Body President. At Sherman, Clark was a star football player and he went on to play football at UCLA. He received his Bachelor's degree at UCLA. During World War II, Clark served in the Navy. Officers in the Navy recognized Clark's intelligence and many talents, and the Navy sent him to the University of St. Louis where he became a medical doctor. After completing medical school and passing his boards, Clark returned to active duty in the Navy as a medical doctor. Frank Clark had a remarkable career, and he continues to practice medicine as a volunteer a few days a week near his home in Woodland, California.

CHAPTER SIX

Navajo Program

Roughly between 1946 and 1961, Sherman Institute offered a special educational space for Navajo Indians or Diné people. The Diné or Navajos as they have come to be known, lived on the largest reservation in the United States, and they boasted a large population living on a rural reservation in Arizona, New Mexico, and Utah. The Navajo Treaty of 1868 had promised Navajo people the first formal education on the newly created reservation. In the treaty, the United States would build a schoolhouse for every 30 students. However, the federal government never lived up to the Navajo Treaty. Over many years, the federal government created only a few schools on the reservation, most of them were on-reservation boarding schools that Navajo parents did not prefer. As a result, few Navajos from rural areas attended schools regularly before World War II, and government officials wished to find a new method of educating Navajo students. As a result, the Office of Indian Education decided to remove children from Dinetah, the Navajo homeland, and their parents. Officials in the Indian Office decided to send Diné students to off-reservation boarding schools. As a result, federal officials decided to create special Navajo Programs on various off-reservation boarding schools where children entered into a new educational space away from home and controlled by federal school officials.

Sherman Institute became one of the sites for the Navajo Program. For over twenty years, the Office of Indian Education only allowed Navajo students to attend Sherman Institute. They excluded most California Indians, much to the chagrin of former students of Sherman who wanted their children to enroll at the boarding school on Magnolia Avenue. Nevertheless, nearly all of the students attending Sherman between 1946 and 1961 were Navajos.

Federal officials designed the curriculum for the Navajo Program, claiming it to be new and unique. Many of the topics and illustrations used in the Navajo Program stemmed from elements of Navajo culture, but overall, the curriculum remained the same at Sherman with a huge emphasis on teaching Navajo children trades and agriculture. Navajo males had greater curricular choices than females who remained stereotyped into courses that would result in low paying positions as hotel maids, house cleaners, seamstresses, short-order cooks, and ironing-washer women. Navajo males could learn to be printers, mechanics, masons, machinists, farmers, ranchers, and other occupations. The Navajo Program offered some academic work in reading, writing, and understanding in the English language. Students also received elementary knowledge of mathematics. But the thrust of the Navajo Program continued the old concepts of assimilation and making Indian students useful laborers in the market economy. To this end, Sherman continued the Outing Program, encouraging Navajo boys and girls to work for wages off campus and encouraging them to join the mainstream workforce of the United States away from reservations.

In addition to education goals of the Office of Indian Education, federal officials wanted to isolate Navajo students to detect and treat tuberculosis. From the late nineteenth century until the 1940s, tuberculosis ravaged many American Indian communities, especially Navajos. Tuberculosis emerged as a severe problem on the Navajo Reservation during the early twentieth century. The Navajo population inhabited a huge geographical area with people living in many remote areas hard to access except by wagons or horseback. As a result, federal health officials could not get a handle on tuberculosis and sought a way to isolate young Navajo students in order to examine them for tuberculosis and conduct regular rechecks in an attempt to control the dangerous disease. Federal officials captured hundreds of Navajo children and over the course of two decades, isolated and removed thousands of Diné students to boarding schools to participate in the special Navajo Program.

Federal superintendents at Sherman Institute took numerous photographs of students during the years of the Navajo Program. Many of these photographs contain captions embedded in the photographs, saying, "We Love Sherman Institute" or "We Like Taking Showers at Sherman Institute." These and other photographs of the Navajo Program provided a portion of the print propaganda produced by the Indian Office to encourage further funding for a unique educational program specifically

> "In the treaty, the United States would build a schoolhouse for every 30 students. However, the federal government never lived up to the Navajo Treaty."

designed to train Navajo boys and girls. The Office of Indian Education claimed it offered a brand new program through the Navajo Program that offered a new form of education. Program leaders insinuated the Navajo Program did not emphasize assimilation, but the curriculum for the program includes a great deal of the old assimilation materials. School officials directed the curriculum to Navajo people and culture, but it remained much the same as in the past with an emphasis of vocational education and employment opportunities in cities away from the Navajo Reservation.

The Special Navajo Program that began in 1946 corresponded to national policies of termination and relocation. The termination policy of the United States provided for the severing of legal ties between the federal government and tribal governments. By eliminating the legal bond between the two nations, the United States destroyed reservations and tribal governments. By eliminating the legal bond between the two nations, the United

States destroyed reservations and recognition of Indian tribes and peoples as Native Americans under the laws of the United States. Thousands of indigenous people, especially Navajos, from the reservation to urban areas to work as laborers. Officials in the Office of Indian Education also supported the all-Navajo Program at Sherman Institute in an effort to examine large numbers of Navajo students infected with tuberculosis, which remained a scourge of Navajo people throughout the era into the 1970s. The Navajo Program remains one component of Sherman's past unknown to most people, but the rich photographic collection at the Sherman Indian Museum graphically depicts a significant era and element of the school's past.

•••

We Like School at SHERMAN INSTITUTE

6.1. Sherman administrators hired professional photographers to snap pictures of studious students participating in the Navajo Program. Sherman officials and the Indian Office also hired Navajo teachers and aids as part of the Navajo Program. School officials used photographs like this to promote the program and show that Navajo students enjoyed their time away from home and that the Navajo Program was working to educate and assimilate Navajo people. As propaganda, photographers placed quaint messages on the photographs, including "We Like School at Sherman Institute" or "We Like to Take Showers at Sherman Institute." These clear messages appear on several photographs associated with the Navajo program. Notice the scene of Navajo horses in the picture behind the instructor.

County Fair Exhibit

6.2. After World War II, the Bureau of Indian Affairs began the Special Five Year Navajo Program. Policy makers of the United States believed the federal government had not fulfilled its obligation to educate Navajos who lived on an expansive reservation about the size of the state of West Virginia. Also, the Medical Division of the Indian Office had not sufficiently arrested tuberculosis on the Navajo Reservation. In order to educate Navajo students and isolate them to diagnose tuberculosis, policy makers created the Navajo Program, sending hundreds of Navajo children to off-reservation boarding schools. Between 1946 and 1961, Sherman Institute admitted only Navajo students and basically used Navajo-specific curriculum to assimilate students. Each year, Sherman provided an exhibit, like the one shown here from the Riverside County Fair, which informed the public about the Navajo Program. Note the sign, "Special Navajo Program, Sherman Institute, Riverside, California."

6.3. Photographers working for the Indian Bureau took many pictures of the Special Navajo Program at Sherman Institute. They used these photographs to "sell" the program to Navajo parents and grandparents as well as the Congress, which appropriated funds of the boarding school. This photograph depicts three male Navajo students and two females who participated in the special Navajo program. The photographer posed these Navajo students in front of the Main School Building at Sherman Institute.

6.4. Because of the special circumstances that brought Navajo students to Sherman Institute, the school administration and officials in Washington, D. C., allowed married students to attend Sherman Institute. Navajo couples and families participated in the educational program, much like married students that attend colleges today. This photograph illustrates this fact. Shown here is a young Navajo family with the parents proudly caring for their baby boy. Navajo families lived on campus.

6.5. The Bureau of Indian Affairs established the Special Navajo Program with many goals. One goal included the teaching of English. The program de-emphasized the Navajo language. Nearly all the Navajo boys and girls attending school at Sherman spoke Navajo as their first language. Policy makers wanted to teach the English language to each student and force him or her to speak only English on campus, a policy that did not work. Navajo students learned English but they did not abandon Dine Bizaad, the Navajo language.

6.6. Teachers made a point of teaching English to students studying at Sherman in the Navajo Program. In this photograph, Navajo boys learn English by watching local television. The photograph was taken in a dorm on the Sherman campus where one television was available to students in the dorm lobby. Officials of the Bureau of Indian Affairs justified the purchase and use of televisions by arguing they taught students the English language.

6.7. The professional photographers hired by the administration at Sherman Institute continually shot photographs that depicted students enjoying their boarding school days. This image depicts older Navajo girls at Sherman making and sharing fry bread with younger Navajo girls, perhaps new arrivals to the campus. In this staged photograph a caption or commentary indicates in English that these students enjoyed living at Sherman. According to Ella Damon, when Navajos make fry bread, they add baking soda, which makes the bread fluffier than many forms of the bread.

Life at Sherman

6.8. During the years of the Special Navajo Program, three Navajo girls learned to cook on a modern stove, including one girl with a hand beater. In 1946, officials of the Bureau of Indian Affairs announced a totally new program for Navajo students, saying that the days of assimilation and civilization had ended at the off-reservation American Indian boarding schools. In reality, the old system of teaching assimilation and forcing students to speak English continued at Sherman, although some teachers and aides spoke Navajo and helped students adjust to the school's curriculum that encouraged all students to speak and read English. Thus, in the Domestic Science classes, Sherman women learned their lessons in English and these courses emphasized childcare and homemaking—just like the old curriculum before World War II.

6.9. With a picture of George Washington and Abraham Lincoln looking on, a teacher reads to Navajo students. The curriculum at Sherman Institute was always presented in English, and teachers used many techniques to encourage Native American students to read in the English language. In this photograph, a Sherman teacher reads a book to young children to peak their interest in reading storybooks of many genres. Throughout its history, Sherman teachers and administrators discouraged student use of Indian languages.

We Like to SWIM, SKATE, BATHE, READ and WRITE LETTERS

6.10. "We Like to Swim, Skate, Bathe, Read and Write Letters at Sherman Institute." Sherman teachers used this and other similar photographs to teach Navajo students how to read. Navajo students of all ages at Sherman Institute enjoyed looking at and studying photographs. Teachers at Sherman used photographs to help Native American students understand the meaning of English words, especially when language barriers existed between the instructor and student. During the years of the Navajo Program, nearly all of the students spoke Navajo as their first language and lessons in English proved very difficult. In addition, school officials used photographs as propaganda, to ensure others that the school cared for and nurtured Native American students. Officials at Sherman Institute used the picture shown here and similar photographs to promote their school and receive additional funding for providing effective and humane education to Native students.

6.11. For many reasons, administrators at Sherman Institute established a bank on campus. As part of the national effort to assimilate Indians, non-Indians taught Indian students the use and value of money. They wanted Native students to join the market economy and learn materialism, an important element of capitalism. At Sherman Institute, the school bank helped Navajo students learn to use a bank by establishing savings accounts, depositing money, and withdrawing funds. Navajo students earned money by working away from campus in the Outing Program. School officials urged students to save money.

6.12. Teachers at Sherman Institute during the era of the Navajo Program taught children civics, a course of study that made students more familiar with the federal system of government of the United States. Teachers instructed young people about the different levels of government within the country, but they did not offer instructions on the ways tribal governments functioned before or after the Indian Reorganization Act of the New Deal Era. In addition, teachers taught Native American students how the branches of government work together to pass laws. In this photograph, a young boy is explaining to other students "how a bill becomes a law."

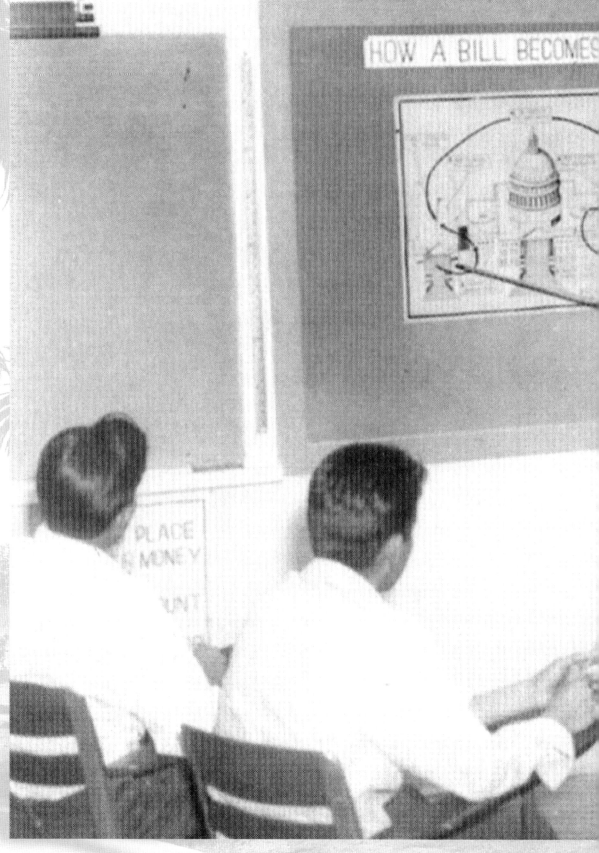

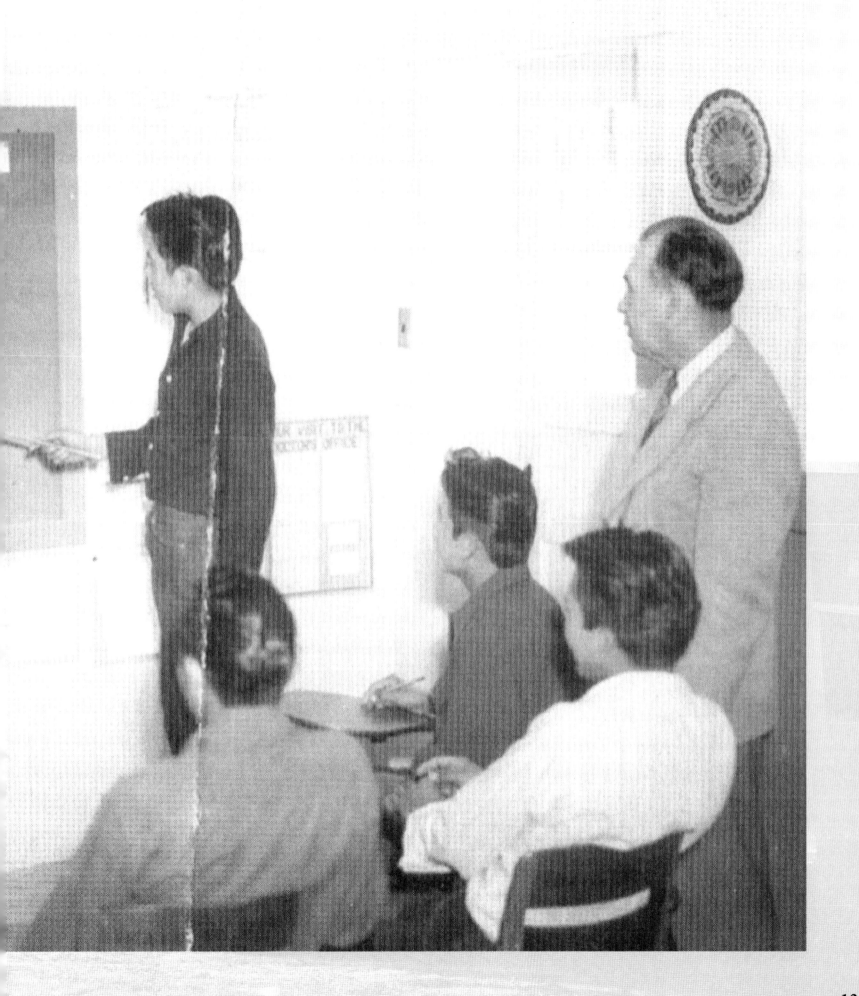

6.13. From the opening of Sherman Institute in 1902, school superintendents and teachers encouraged students to participate in the school's social functions, which served to "civilize" Native American children. Social gatherings were part of some classes within the United States, and instructors taught Sherman students the proper way to set up and execute a formal dance. After World War II, students in the Navajo Program held formal social events such as dances and parties. This photograph depicts students enjoying a formal dance held in the Sherman gymnasium, complete with colorful decorations.

6.14. The Domestic Science courses at Sherman Institute taught Sherman women how to care for children and households with the objective of creating good mothers and talented maids. Sherman females from the Navajo tribe had to take a course of study in Home Economics, and the curriculum always emphasized the ability to cook a meal and present it properly on the table. Teachers taught Sherman women "civilized" manners and proper etiquette so they could serve their own family and others. As part of the curriculum, students in Domestic Science had to serve other students. In this photograph, a student of Home Economics prepares to serve their fellow students from the Nursing Program.

6.15. As part of the school's effort to "civilize" and Christianize Native American students, school officials encourage students to celebrate the Christmas season. This photograph depicts Navajo students engaging in a gift exchange at Christmas. This tradition continues on the Navajo Reservation today. During the Christmas Season of 1976, the faculty in the Department of History and Navajo Studies exchanged gifts. Students in this photograph participate in hanging Christmas stockings on a "chimney." In the Navajo language, they greeted each other with Ya'at'eeh Keshmesh or Merry Christmas.

CHAPTER SEVEN

Architecture and Built Environment

The federal government planned the construction of Sherman Institute at the opening of the twentieth century, and both school officials and Riverside elites wanted the school built in the Mission Revival architectural style found elsewhere in the city, especially at the Mission Inn Hotel. Officials of the Indian Office built Sherman Institute in the wake of the nineteenth century and beginning of the twentieth century when Southern California experienced a wave of romanticism surrounding the Spanish colonial era. Promoters of Southern California followed the lead of novelist Helen Hunt Jackson who popularized the region and the Spanish mission system in her best-selling book, Ramona. Like many areas of California, the American Southwest, and some in the Southeast, Spanish missionaries had established Catholic missions to convert Native Americans to the Christian faith.

After secularization of the missions in 1834, Spanish missions fell into disrepair as Mexican Californios took over large land grants where they raised thousands of longhorn cattle on the lush, natural rangelands of Southern California. In the twenty-one missions of California, Indians became the vaqueros on the many ranchos dotting the landscape. California Indians had adapted to a new life under Mexican rule when American soldiers, settlers, and state builders arrived during the Mexican-American War, 1846-1848. Much of the architecture of California resembled that of Northern Mexico, Arizona, and New Mexico. Builders created most buildings from adobe bricks and other natural materials found in the area. Spanish priests used Indian labor to build mission buildings, including the churches. The architecture of mission churches and buildings influenced a romantic new architecture that drew on the old missions but missed its mark in the realm of authenticity.

> "Thus, Sherman is not an historic artifact of the past. It is a living institution to many American Indian people..."

In the late nineteenth century, Indian reformers and promoters of California created an idealized image of the Spanish era and mission system. During the mid-nineteenth century and following the United States-Mexican War, boosters of California created a new and romantic image of the Spanish mission system and heritage. Promoters of California put a new and positive slant to the mission era, especially the architecture. In addition, boosters downplayed the power and sovereignty of California Indians and cast Native Californians as slow, lazy, docile, and unintelligent people that lived a pleasurable and complacent life at the missions. By the end of the nineteenth century, promoters and writers also initiated a new architectural style that had limited relationship to the mission adobe structures. Protestants from the United States had condemned the Spanish Mission system of the Franciscan Order of the Catholic Church. Initially, many settlers from the United States spread negative propaganda about Catholicism and the missions.

By the late nineteenth century, architects of the era created a new style of architecture that became known as the Mission Revival, Neo Spanish Colonial, or Mission architectural style. It represented the mythical past and glorious mission era of California's past. The style was not accurate or authentic, but it was popular at the time the Indian Office built Sherman Institute and it remains popular today. In 1900, Indian Education officials decided to build Sherman Institute in the new Spanish Revival style. Frank Miller, a successful businessman and political force in Riverside, had decided to build the Glenwood Mission Inn in the Mission Revival style. He encouraged the Indian Office to build the Indian School on Magnolia Avenue in the same architectural style, thereby reaffirming the myth that his Hotel had once been a Spanish mission connected to the large number of Indians being schooled at Sherman. Miller's Mission Inn still stands in Riverside, California, and remains and icon of Southern California.

Architects worked on the building plans and elevations of Sherman Institute. They planned on building classrooms, dorms, shops, and administrative buildings in the new Mission style. Some of the most striking photographs found in the collection at Sherman Indian Museum depict the magnificent buildings at Sherman Institute. School superintendents, teachers, and students carefully documented the built environment of Sherman through numerous engaging images. Construction crews created buildings that appeared to be made of massive adobe, but they constructed the buildings primarily with bricks, blocks, wood, and stucco.

The main classrooms, administration building, auditorium, hospital, shops, dormitories, and most other buildings on campus reflected the Mission Revival style. From the photographs, it appears that the faculty and staff housing was not built in the Mission Revival style. Architects planned faculty and staff housing in simple rectangular dwellings, a fact verified by Sherman historian Galen Townsend who grew up in faculty housing. Most of the original buildings of Sherman Institute, created in the Mission Revival style, stood beautifully and proudly on the south side of Magnolia Avenue until the 1970s when government officials decided to destroy the old buildings. They claimed the buildings were not fit to experience an earthquake, and they argued it would cost more to retrofit Sherman Institute than to knock down the buildings. As a result, the Bureau of Indian Affairs chose to level the old buildings to the ground. Only a few of the original buildings remain at Sherman today, including the shops and administrative building, which houses the Sherman Indian Museum. But a spirit of bygone days remains on campus as does a sincere attachment of many Native Americans and non-Indians to the Indian School on Magnolia Avenue.

Thus, Sherman is not an historic artifact of the past. It is a living institution to many American Indian people and non-Native

Americans who continue to have a relationship with Sherman School Museum. Each year, hundreds of people visit the museum, some of who research the old institute and their relatives who attended school in Riverside. Contemporary students still walk the grounds of Sherman Indian High School, the same Sherman byways traveled since 1902 by thousands of Native American students.

•••

7.1. This photograph is extremely rare. From the air, a photographer took a picture of several Sherman students standing by the flagpole spelling out Sherman Institute. The image and formation of the students took a great deal of time and effort to get this correct, but the result is a part of the built environment at Sherman, using human beings to form the school name near the flagpole. The flagpole stands in the same place today, although a new pole recently replaced the old one.

7.2. Centered between two tall palm trees (both planted in 1901 and still on campus), the American flag flies in front of the Main Building at Sherman Institute. Superintendent Harwood Hall built the Main School Building in 1901. At the base of this building, officials placed the first cornerstone at Sherman. At the same time, school officials buried a time capsule that contemporary people opened in 2002. The box and its contents are on display today at Sherman Indian Museum.

7.3. The Main Building at Sherman Institute stood as a beacon to American civilization and assimilation. Superintendent Harwood Hall, Riverside entrepreneur Frank Miller, and officials of the Office of Indian Affairs planned for the multi-story Main Building at Sherman Institute to be an impressive symbol of the United States and its campaign to Americanize the indigenous students of the country. Sherman was the flagship of all the off-reservation American Indian Boarding schools and the built environment left a lasting impression for all that saw the original buildings. The Main Building at Sherman Institute stood in front of the parade ground and was the most prominent building on campus. Magnolia Avenue ran east and west in front of the Main Building, and students entered the institution from Magnolia Avenue. From the street looking south, students saw a driveway running south up an incline dotted with date palm trees and the flagpole. Beyond the American flag, students saw this impressive building along the horizon.

7.4. [Above] This is one of the iconic symbols used in past publications depicting Sherman Institute and the Sherman Braves. Past and present students of the campus treasure the fact that they are part of the on-going history of the Indian School on Magnolia Avenue.

7.5. [Below] Sherman's story belongs to the past, present, and future. American Indian students, including the two twirlers and two pompom girls, lived and participated in life on the Sherman campus. From their faces, it appears they found joy participating with the school band, and they represented many students that did not succumb to the pressures of forced assimilation. Like many more students, they survived their boarding school seasons. Students used their Sherman days to turn the power. They retained their Native identity and enhanced the lives of their people. Each year at the school's reunion, students sing to honor Sherman alumni. The alums sing the Sherman Fight Song and remember their time, for better or worse, at Sherman Institute.

7.6. The Main Building and surrounding buildings dominated the campus of Sherman Institute. Looking south and east, this view of the major buildings at Sherman also provides an image of the marching band and a group of marching Sherman cadets. During the early years of Sherman Institute, all Native American children had to dress in a military uniform. This policy originated in 1879 at Carlisle Indian Industrial School where Superintendent Richard Henry Pratt, previously a captain in the United States Army, designed the first off-reservation American Indian boarding school as a military school. This tradition continued at all the boarding schools where disciples of Pratt forced young children to dress like little cadets. In this early photograph, students were dressed in military uniforms and marched past the school band on the parade ground in front of the main school building at Sherman.

7.7. When the Japanese bombed Pearl Harbor on December 7, 1941, "a day that will live in infamy," many Native Americans volunteered to fight for the United States. American Indian men and women enlisted in the armed forces and even more worked in the war industries and bought War Bonds to support the war effort. Martin Napa, for example, joined the elite group of Navajo Code Talkers. Napa fought and was highly decorated for his efforts during the Battles of Iwo Jima, Marshall Islands, Tinnian, and the Marianas. Former combat Marine Dillon Story remarked, "the Code Talkers saved thousands of lives." During World War II, thirty-eight former students from Sherman Institute died fighting and many more, like Napa, were wounded. In 1942, Sherman honored all servicemen and servicewomen with Sherman's own War Memorial situated near the flagpole and between two prominent palm trees that still stand on the grounds of Sherman Indian High School. Contemporary people wish to erect a memorial to the many Sherman students who fought and died for the United States.

7.8. The photographer took this picture from up the street from the Sherman Hospital. Several student nurses trained at the Sherman Hospital at Sherman Institute. When students became ill or injured themselves in accidents, they went to the Sherman Hospital for first aid and medical care. The nursing program offered a rigorous program at Sherman when the school first opened, and it existed at the school for many years. Student nurses helped doctors and nurses fight tuberculosis, pneumonia, and influenza. When they graduated, they often took their training back to their homes to serve their people.

supt's. Residence

7.9. In 1901 and 1902, Superintendent Harwood Hall and his wife, Frances, oversaw the construction of the Superintendent's Residence on the campus. It was built in the Mission Revival style. From 1902 until 1970, the Indian Office provided the headmaster and his family with a dwelling that included built-in sleeping porches the family used during the hot summer months. This was home to several superintendents and some students considered it an honor to visit this home on special occasions.

7.10. Various employees of Sherman Institute took up residence in these wood framed buildings. These buildings, located on the periphery of the main campus, were not built in the Mission Revival style. Many of the Sherman Brats grew up in these dwellings, including Tonita Largo and Galen Townsend.

7.11. Several dormitories existed at Sherman Institute, including the Tepee Dorm shown in this photograph. Like all the dorms at Sherman, the Tepee was built in the Mission Revival style. Dormitory residents formed a bond with each other, creating intermural teams and participating in other school events as a group.

7.12. This photograph depicts Wigwam Dorm, one of several dorms at Sherman Institute for male students. The dormitories were an integral part of the built environment at Sherman, and school officials built all of the old buildings in the Mission Revival style. This photograph depicts Alessandro, a boys dorm at Sherman Institute named after a character in Helen Hunt Jackson's Ramona. Notice the basketball backboard and hoop near the palm trees toward the left center of the photograph.

7.13. [Above] This is a photograph of the Minnehaha Home or dormitory. It was a girl's dorm, and the name derived from the heroine of the poem by Henry David Longfellow who wrote the "Song of Hiawatha." A man named Hiawatha was a historical figure among the Onondaga people. He and the Peace Maker brought together the Haudenosaunee or Iroquois Confederacy. Longfellow's Hiawatha and Minnehaha are fictional figures among the Ojibwe, also known as Annishinabe or Chippewa. Many of the dormitories at Sherman Institute looked similar, as school officials created all of them in the Mission Revival style. Superintendent Harwood Hall designed all the dormitories to look similar or alike to standardize the housing units and keep down construction costs.

7.14. [Below] The young women at Sherman Institute took great pride in being part of a dormitory community. The girls pose in front of their dormitory, built in the Mission Revival style, wearing white dresses. Each year, photographers took images of students from particular dormitories. The students in this photograph not only lived together, but they worked as a team to clean their dormitory and provide for the upkeep of the building and each room. Some dormitories also cultivated and planted their own gardens, and they competed together in intermural sports. Notice that some of the young women have long hair while others have their hair trimmed short.

7.15. This is a photograph of the Farm House or School House at the Sherman Farm located west of the Main Campus on Indiana Street about five miles. The photographer took this picture just before the school demolished the building. The caption on the photograph reads "School house at Farm November 21, 1934." The building was condemned and was scheduled to be knocked down. Notice the farm's water tower in the background. The photographer took this photograph on the day after a camera shot a picture of Sherman boys digging an irrigation canal. Perhaps school officials used federal dollars of the Sherman Economic Recovery Act (SERA) to demolish this building and a government photographer captured the image.

7.16. At 8:22 AM on March 28, 1940, a photographer took this picture of a classroom at Sherman Institute. The students in this image are engaged in "Proper Letter Writing." Most likely, they are attending an English class and are depicted busy at work with the sun beaming in from the east side of the room. A picture of President Calvin Coolidge looks on above on one blackboard. On the blackboard to the back of the room, the teacher has inscribed "An American Proverb" as a thought piece for the students. The proverb reads: "The world is a pair of stairs. Some go up and some go down." The message is clear. The teacher wanted students to take the stairway up to a higher level.

7.17. This is the dairy barn located on the extreme southern end of the campus. The barn no longer exists, as Highway 91 replaced the site and removed the soil where the Sherman Dairy once stood. Each morning and evening a group of boys (and sometimes girls as well) milked the cows of the dairy herd at Sherman Institute. The cows produced more milk than the students at Sherman could consume, so superintendents sold excess milk to local distributors. The money helped support the school. Students made cheese, cottage cheese, and other milk products with milk from the Sherman Dairy.

7.18. The photograph depicts girls planting a small garden, which was part of the curriculum. Male and female students at Sherman Institute planted, tended, weeded, and harvested truck gardens. They used aged manure from turkeys, chickens, geese, goats, sheep, pigs, horses, and cattle to enrich the soil. Students harvested their crops and ate vegetables grown at Sherman. When the school cafeteria had a surplus of fruits, vegetables, or meat, superintendents sold excess produce and meats to grocers in Riverside.

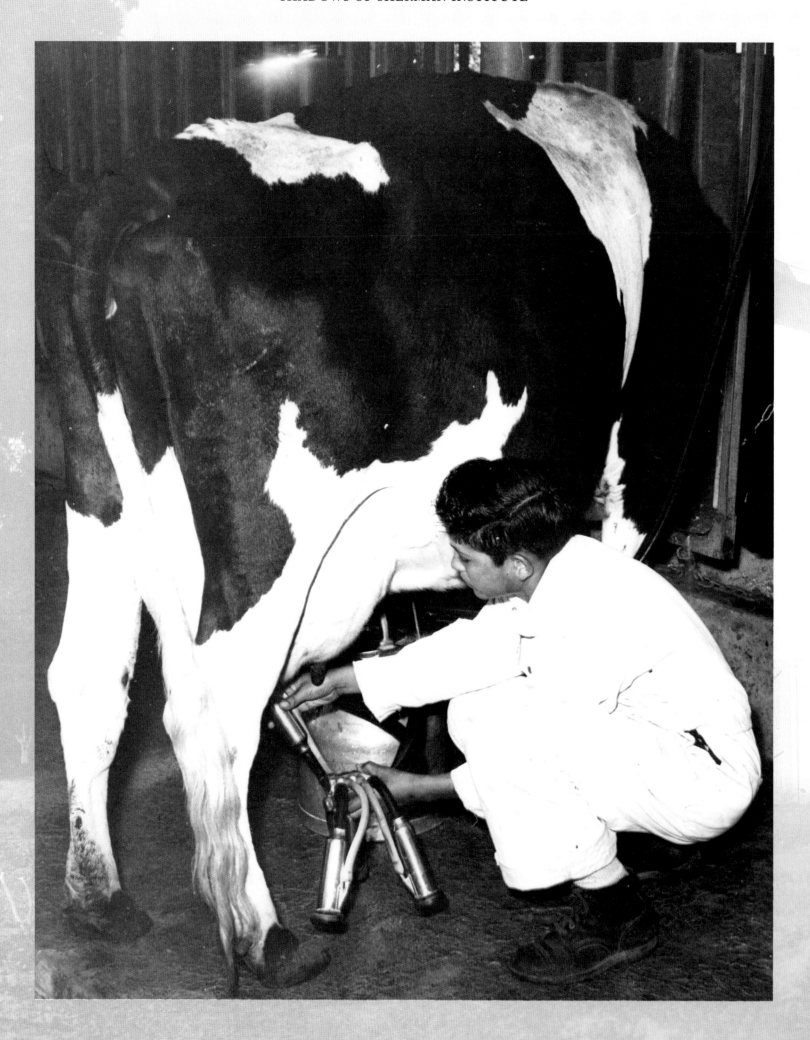

7.19. Originally, boys at Sherman Institute hand milked cows at the Sherman Dairy twice a day, which was a great deal of work and tired the boy's hands. School officials placed the school dairy south of campus where Highway 91 now cuts through the south side of Sherman Indian High School. Student workers milked the cows each day and transported the milk in large cans to the cafeteria and to stations where milk wagons picked up the raw milk to sell in Riverside and surrounding cities. This photograph was taken after the invention of milking machines. It shows a boy fitting milking implements to a cow's teats so machines could milk them rather than hand milking.

7.20. This is a rare group photograph of boys and girls working together at the Sherman Dairy Farm of Sherman Institute. The group picture shows boys and girls with a pail in one hand and a milking stool in the other. A teacher stands to the left. Notice the girls and boys wear white uniforms and carry pails they will use to collect milk. Sherman officials used milk and milk products made by students in the school cafeteria. They sold excess milk to local businesses or schools.

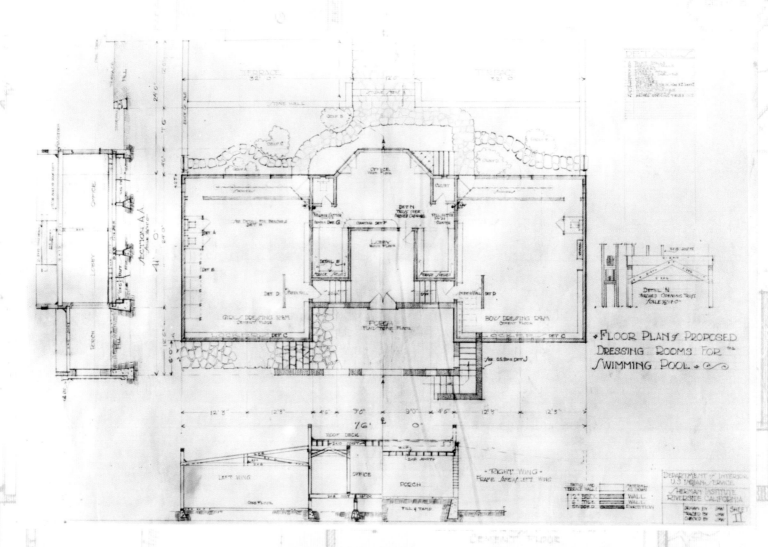

7.21. Policy makers placed Sherman Institute in sunny Southern California where the summers are hot and winter months mild. For many years, Sherman did not have a school swimming pool but received funding to build a pool in the 1930s. Only a few plans exist for the built environment of Sherman Institute. This is one of the few remaining construction plans for the Indian school. These plans are for the Dressing Rooms for boys and girls at the school's swimming pool. The plans are preserved still in the archival collection at Sherman Institute Museum.

7.22. With a team of mules and shovels, these boys began construction of the swimming pool and dressing rooms at Sherman. They built the swimming pool near the present site of the water tower at Sherman Indian High School. The modern swimming pool provided hours of fun for students, and an opportunity for students to learn to swim and compete in races. When construction began on the swimming pool, students shared the great excitement of having a place to swim on their campus during the hot summers of Riverside.

S-E-R-A Workers
Installing Irrigation System

Sherman Institute
Nov. 20-1934

7.23. Sherman Institute received federal funds during the Great Depression. Federal funds channeled into the Sherman Economic Recovery Act (SERA), perhaps part of the Works Project Administration (WPA). In any case, this photograph depicts Sherman students digging irrigation ditches on campus. They built some ditches on campus but these boys also worked through the program off campus in different locales. They earned low wages for their labor, but they received great "experience." Sometimes superintendents sent part of their earnings home to their parents during the hard times of the Depression. A photographer took this picture on November 20, 1934.

Indian School, Sherman Institute, Riverside, Cal.

944:—Indian School, Sherman Institute, Riverside, Cal.

7.24. [Above] Sherman Institute became a tourist attraction for Southern California in general and Riverside, California, in particular. Tourists visiting the Mission Inn and other hotels in the area often traveled to Sherman Institute where young Native American students gave visitors a tour of the campus and allowed tourists to take their pictures. This was part of the promotional efforts of school superintendents to popularize the assimilation work at Sherman and provide potential political support for the school. Sherman administrators had post cards made of the Indian School on Magnolia Avenue to sell to visitors. This is one image placed on post cards.

7.25. [Below] This image emerges from an early post card depicting, "Indian School, Sherman Institute, Riverside, Cal." It offers a similar view as the photograph of the Main Building and Parade Ground. The Sherman gift shop sold post cards of the school to visitors taking tours of the campus.

7.26. This image provides "Early Air View of Campus." The photograph offers an overview of the Sherman Campus in 1930. The built environment is extensive, and by the era of the Great Depression, the campus included several trees, shrubs, and flowers. Notice the surrounding area to Sherman Institute, which was once rural and agricultural.

7.27. This is an aerial view of Sherman Institute circa 1950. The photographer took this shot from the south facing north with Magnolia Avenue toward the upper part of the school. Harwood Hall cited the Sherman Dairy, poultry coups, and other animals on the south side of the main campus, which is seen here in the foreground. Notice the circle in the middle of the photograph, which features the driveway onto campus from Magnolia Avenue and the flagpole. The image provides an understanding of the rural nature of area surrounding Sherman Institute with citrus and other agriculture.

7.28. After years of neglect, the government paid to cut, carve, and erect a large black headstone with the names of several Sherman students who paid the full measure of attending boarding school, dying in the process. The off-reservation boarding school experience took the lives of too many indigenous students, including school children attending Sherman. When school administrators could not send their bodies home, they buried the dead at Sherman's cemetery. Students also used cement to create headstones for the dead. In 2008, Southern Paiute Salt Song Singers, including former student body president Matthew Hanks Leivas, conducted a mourning ceremony at the school cemetery. Salt Song Singers sang for the students and prayed that their souls would, in the words of one tribal elder, "go on to the light and not hang around the cemetery and mountains here."

7.29. All of the off-reservation American Indian boarding schools had cemeteries. School officials buried students on campuses when they could not ship their bodies home. This is a photograph of the dedication of the large black headstone at Sherman's school cemetery with the names of several fallen students carved into the stone. The photograph and memorial are reminders of the deaths suffered by Sherman students while going to school. Some students died of diseases, others by accidents. School officials created a cemetery at the Sherman farm off Indiana Avenue in Riverside, California, about five miles from the main campus. Students at Sherman built coffins, made headstones, and buried their fellow classmates. Parents, grandparents, and tribal elders did not sing the children into the next world, but officials provided Christian burials. Early in the twenty-first century, the Pechanga Tribe of Luiseño Indians bought new headstones for each person buried at the cemetery. Today, current students at Sherman Indian High School care for the cemetery.

7.30. Over the course of many years, several people have donated their time to preserve the history of Sherman Institute. Blossom Hathaway, Lorene Sisquoc, and Cindi Alvitre are three of the many volunteers that have worked at the Sherman Indian Museum, helping to preserve and protect the rich historical past of Sherman. Notice that behind these three Native American women leaders are the black albums holding many of the photographs that appear in this volume. Museum volunteers plan to scan every photograph in the collection and provide further protection to the precious photographic collection.

Conclusion

In 1970, the Bureau of Indian Affairs ended the Sherman Institute. In its place, the Office of Indian Education renamed the institute Sherman Indian High School. Officials in the Bureau of Indian Affairs kept the new high school on the grounds of Sherman Institute, but fear of the old buildings being unsafe in an earthquake led federal officials to destroy the old campus and rebuild a new campus for the high school on the old school grounds of Sherman Institute. As a result, federal authorities demolished most of the old buildings created in the Mission Revival style and replaced them with single story stucco buildings with far less character or meaning. Since the fall of 1970, Sherman Indian High School has stood on a portion of the old school grounds that had once housed Sherman Institute. Officials removed the barns and animals on the main campus, and construction of the 91 Freeway from Riverside to Orange County cut a swath through the lands that had once held the main dairy barn and pasture lands. The site of the old water tower remains, proudly announcing Sherman Indian High.

Much has changed from its opening in 1902, but Sherman Indian High School remains a significant resource for members of the Native American communities of the United States. Sherman remains one of the few off-reservation American Indian boarding schools still functioning today. Some people may view Sherman as anachronistic, but many contemporary Native Americans, especially alum, feel strongly that Sherman Indian High School has an important role to play in the twenty-first century. Sherman offers American Indian students and parents a choice, a site where American Indian students may assemble to learn many subjects including first-hand Native American Studies from teachers, counselors, dormitory representatives, and faculty. Through its own historical museum and museum preservation program, students at Sherman Indian High School enjoy the luxury of having highly significant historical documents about the school's history located on their own campus. High school students attending Sherman today have the opportunity of being a part of the museum through internships. Students attending Sherman Indian High School may intern in a successful museum program and learn more about the academic field known as Public History.

Through Sherman Indian Museum, high school students learn to lead tours, arrange archival collections, plan exhibits, interpret using material culture, establish historical programs, and care for thousands of unique photographs. The photographic collection at Sherman Institute is substantial, and neither Native Americans nor members of the general public have ever seen the dynamic photographs housed at the museum. Sherman students have a unique opportunity to work with talented volunteers, museum professionals, university students, researchers, and professors to preserve pictures and documents about the Sherman experience. For many students, the Sherman Indian Museum and its cultural programs are a highlight of their high school educations, bringing them closer to former students and past times. This historical connection reaches back to 1902 when Superintendent Harwood Hall opened the doors to Sherman to the first students. For over one hundred years, Sherman has offered Native Americans new forms of education and knowledge about how they could "turn the power" and put their formal educations to work to benefit Native American people.

In many ways and for many years, the Sherman Indian Museum has pointed the way into the future for American Indian students. In order for contemporary Sherman students to be successful, they must have a firm understanding of the past. The museum protects that knowledge through its many sources and reminds everyone that at one point in our nation's history, policy makers encouraged the destruction of American Indian cultures, religions, families, foods, arts, and languages. Not so long ago, the United States discriminated against indigenous people and stole their freedom to live out their lives as they wished. Sherman Institute stood as a monument to forced assimilation and Christianization. Over the course of many years, American Indian educational policies have changed dramatically. Some things have remained the same. For many students, staff, and faculty associated with Sherman, the Indian School on Magnolia Avenue will always remain a site of multiple meanings and a site of profound significance to the nation and to the indigenous people of the United States and beyond.

Notes

INTRODUCTION

1. In 1970, the Bureau of Indian Affairs and its Office of Indian Education situated Sherman Indian High School on the old school grounds of Sherman Institute, located on Magnolia Avenue in Riverside, California. For the first comprehensive history of Sherman Institute, see Diana Meyers Bahr, *The Students of Sherman Institute: Education and Native Identity Since 1892* (Norman: University of Oklahoma Press, 2014).

2. "Career Opportunity Brochure," Sherman Institute, Collections of the Sherman Indian Museum, 9010 Magnolia Avenue, Riverside, California, 92503.

3. Jon Ille, "A Curriculum for Social Change: The Special Navajo Five Year Program, 1946-1961," in Clifford E. Trafzer, Matthew Sakiestewa Gilbert, and Lorene Sisquoc, editors, *The Indian School on Magnolia Avenue: Voices and Images From Sherman Institute* (Corvallis: Oregon State University Press, 2012), 137-158.

4. Patricia Dixon and Clifford E. Trafzer, "The Place of American Indian Boarding Schools in Contemporary Society," in Clifford E. Trafzer, Jean A. Keller, and Lorene Sisquoc, editors, *Boarding School Blues: Revisiting American Indian Educational Experiences* (Lincoln: University of Nebraska Press, 2006), 232-242.

5. Trafzer, Keller, and Sisquoc, "Introduction," in Trafzer, Keller, and Sisquoc, *Boarding School Blues*, 5-6.

6. Karen Swisher, "Education," in Duane Champagne, editor, *The Native North American Almanac* (Detroit: Gale Researchers, 1994), 855-857.

7. The most recent and significant works on the mission system in California includes James Sandos, "Junípero Serra's Canonization and the Historical Record," *American Historical Review* 93 (December 1988), 1253-1269; George H. Phillips, *Vineyards and Vaqueros: Indian Labor and the Economic Expansion of Southern California, 1771-1877* (Norman: Arthur H. Clark and University of Oklahoma Press, 2010); and Steven Hackel, *Junípero Serra: California's Founding Father* (New York: Hill and Wang, 2013).

8. On March 13, 2015, the California Center for Native Nations held a symposium, "California Indians, Canonization of Junípero Serra, and Consequences of Colonialism" during which panels of California Indians and scholars exchanged their interpretations of Father Serra and the Spanish mission system in California. Professor Angela D'Arcy Mooney and the Sacred Places Institute for Indigenous Peoples are producing a documentary, "Living in the Shadow of Father Serra," which will feature interviews and elements of the symposium on Serra's canonization.

9. David Wallace Adams, *Education for Extinction: American Indians and the Boarding School Experience* (Lawrence: University Press of Kansas, 1995), 36-44.

10. Ibid.; Trafzer, Keller, and Sisquoc, eds., *Boarding School Blues*, 13-15; Robert Engs, *Educating the Disfranchised and Disinherited: Samuel Chapman Armstrong and Hampton Institute, 1839-1893* (Knoxville: University of Tennessee Press, 1999).

11. Richard Henry Pratt, "The Advantages of Mingling Indians with Whites," *Proceedings of the National Conference of Charities and Corrections, 1892,* 46; for a greater insight into Pratt, see his book edited by Robert M. Utley, *Battlefield and Classroom: Four Decades with American Indians, 1867-1904* (New Haven: Yale University Press, 1964).

12. Pratt, "The Advantages of Mingling Indians with Whites," 46.

13. Adams, *Education for Extinction*, 97-111, 125, 138-144, 258-259.

14. Luther Standing Bear, *My People, The Sioux* (Lincoln: University of Nebraska Press, reprint, 1975), 123, 130-132, 140-142, 187; Trafzer, Keller, and Sisquoc, "Introduction," in Trafzer, Keller, and Sisquoc, eds., *Boarding School Blues*, 15.

15. Standing Bear, *My People, The Sioux*, 124.

16. Oral interview of Rita Coosewoon by Clifford Trafzer, April 2008, Oklahoma City, Oklahoma; Diana Meyers Bahr, *Viola Martinez, California Paiute* (Norman: University of Oklahoma Press, 2003), 51-65. For information on the role of music at American Indian boarding schools, see Melissa D. Parkhurst, *To Win the Indian Heart: Music at Chemawa Indian School* (Corvallis: Oregon State University Press, 2014).

17. Clifford E. Trafzer and Leleua Loupe, "From Perris Indian School to Sherman Institute," in Trafzer, Gilbert, and Sisquoc, eds., The Indian School on Magnolia Avenue, 19-34; Jean A. Keller, *Empty Beds: Indian Student Health at Sherman Institute, 1902-1922* (East Lansing: Michigan State University Press, 2002), 1-2, 20-27, 114-115, 123, 128, 188.

18. Oral interview of Nathan Gonzales by Clifford E. Trafzer, February 13, 2015, Redlands, California; William O. Medina, "Selling Patriotic Indians at Sherman Institute," in Trafzer, Gilbert, and Sisquoc, eds., *The Indian School on Magnolia Avenue*, 65-80.

19. Robert R. McCoy, "Mission Architecture and Sherman Institute," in Trafzer, Gilbert, and Sisquoc, *The Indian School on Magnolia Avenue*, 35-64. In the same volume, see Trafzer and Loupe, "From Perris to Sherman Institute," 19-22.

20. Ibid.

21. David Wallace Adams provides an excellent overview of the federal American Indian boarding school system in his book, *Education for Extinction*. Adams grew up in Southern California and as a young person, drove by the Sherman Institute, often asking his parents about the separate school for Native American children. His early association with Sherman as a boy led him to research and write on the American Indian boarding school system.

22. Kevin Whalen offers the most comprehensive study of the Outing Program at Sherman Institute, which naturally examines Indian student labor in Southern California.

His work on student working in Los Angeles is a hallmark of his study and the best treatment of Indian labor during the twentieth century. See Whalen, Kevin. "Beyond School Walls: Labor, Mobility, and Indian Education in Southern California, 1900-1940;" Kevin Whalen, *Native Students at Work: American Indian Labor at Sherman Institutes's Outing Program, 1900-1945* (Seattle: University of Washington Press, 2016); "Labored Learning: The Outing System at Sherman Institute, 1902-1930." *American Indian Culture and Research Journal* 36, no. 1 (2012): 151-75.

23. Ibid.
24. Clifford Trafzer obtained this information from Cahuilla elder Robert Levi during the annual Medicine Ways Conference in 1990 at the University of California, Riverside. Levi attended Sherman Institute and later worked at the school for many years.
25. Trafzer and Loupe, "From Perris Indian School to Sherman Institute," 20-21.
26. McCoy, "Mission Architecture and Sherman Institute," 35-64.
27. Trafzer, Gilbert, and Sisquoc, eds., *The Indian School on Magnolia Avenue*, 2-4; Katrina Paxton, "Learning Gender: Female Students at the Sherman Institute, 1907-1925," in Trafzer, Keller, and Sisquoc, eds., *Boarding School Blues*, 174-186.
28. Trafzer, Keller, and Sisquoc, eds., Boarding School Blues, 76, 220-221. Also see recent documentaries on American Indian residential and boarding schools as well as internet web sites about abuse. See also Ward Churchill, *Kill the Indian, Save the Man: The Genocidal Impact of American Indian Residential Schools* (San Francisco: City Lights, 2004).
29. Oral interview of Francis Morongo by Clifford E. Trafzer, Pauline Murillo, and Leleua Loupe, October 9, 2001, San Manuel Indian Reservation, Highland, California.
30. Oral interview of William O. Medina by Clifford E. Trafzer, February 2, 2015, Banning, California.
31. Bahr, *Viola Martinez*, 58-59.
32. Clifford E. Trafzer, editor, *Quechan Indian Voices: Lee Emerson and Patrick Miguel* (Riverside: California Center for Native Nations, University of California, Riverside, 2012), 12, 22-23, 30-32.
33. Ibid.
34. Oral interview of Matthew Hanks Leivas by Clifford E. Trafzer, February 17-19, 2013, Chemehuevi Indian Reservation.
35. Readers of this volume will benefit greatly by examining an excellent overview of boarding schools based on a superior exhibit at the Heard Museum in Phoenix, Arizona. See Margaret L. Archuleta, Brenda J. Child, and Tsianina Lomawaima, *Away From Home: American Indian Boarding School Experiences* (Phoenix: Heard Museum, 2000).
36. Clifford Trafzer met with Lorene Sisquoc and Galen Townsend on March 11, 2015 to discuss the photographic collection at Sherman Indian Museum. At that time, the group consulted about the families that are termed, Sherman Brats, including Sisquoc and Townsend. These two individuals shared a great deal of original information with Trafzer that is included in this work. The author owes a great debt to these two Sherman Brats.

Suggested Readings

Adams, David Wallace. "Beyond Bleakness: The Brighter Side of American Indian Boarding Schools, 1870-1940." In *Boarding School Blues: Revisiting American Indian Educational Experiences*, eds. Clifford E. Trafzer, Jean A. Keller, and Lorene Sisquoc, 35-64. Lincoln: University of Nebraska Press, 2006.

------. Education for Extinction: American Indians and the Boarding School Experience, 1875-1928. Lawrence: University Press of Kansas, 1995.

------. "Education in Hues: Red and Black at Hampton Institute, 1878-1893." *South Atlantic Quarterly* 76 (1977): 159-76.

------. "Fundamental Considerations: The Deep Meaning of Native American Schooling, 1880-1920." *Harvard Educational Review* 58, no. 1 (1988): 1-28.

Ahern, Wilbert. "An Experiment Aborted: Returned Indian Students in the Indian School Service, 1881–1908." *Ethnohistory* 42 (Spring 1997): 263–304.

Amerman, Stephen Kent. *Urban Indians in Phoenix Schools, 1940-2000*. Lincoln: University of Nebraska Press, 2010.

Andrews, Thomas G. "Turning the Tables on Assimilation: Oglala Lakotas and the Pine Ridge Day Schools, 1889-1920s." *Western Historical Quarterly* 33, no. 4 (Winter 2002): 407-430.

Archuleta, Margaret L., Brenda Child, and K. Tsianina Lomawaima, eds. *Away from Home: American Indian Boarding School Experiences*. Phoenix: Heard Museum, 2000.

Bahr, Diana Meyers. *From Mission to Metropolis: Cupeño Indian Women in Los Angeles*. Norman: University of Oklahoma Press, 1993.

------. *The Students of Sherman Indian School: Education and Native Identity Since 1892*. Norman: University of Oklahoma Press, 2014.

------. *Viola Martinez: California Paiute Living in Two Worlds*. Norman: University of Oklahoma Press, 2003.

Basso, Keith. *Wisdom Sits in Places: Landscape and Language among the Western Apache*. Albuquerque: University of New Mexico Press, 1996.

Bauer, Jr., William J. "Round Valley Indian Families at the Sherman Institute, 1900-1945." *Southern California Quarterly* 92, no. 4 (Winter 2010-2011): 393-421.

Berman, Tressa. "'All We Needed Was Our Gardens': Women's Work and Welfare Reform in the Reservation Economy." In *Native Pathways: American Indian Culture and Economic Development in the Twentieth Century*, eds. Brian Hosmer and Colleen O'Neill, 133-155. Boulder: University Press of Colorado, 2004.

Biolsi, Thomas. *Deadliest Enemies: Law and the Making of Race Relations on and off the Rosebud Reservation*. Berkeley and Los Angeles: University of California Press, 2001.

Cahill, Kathleen. "'An Indian Teacher among Indians': Native Women as Federal Employees." In *Indigenous Women and Work: From Labor to Activism*, ed. Carol Williams, 210-24. Urbana: University of Illinois Press, 2012.

------. *Federal Fathers and Mothers: A Social History of the United States Indian Service, 1869-1933*. Chapel Hill: University of North Carolina Press, 2011.

Carney, Michael Carey. *Native American Higher Education in the United States*. New Brunswick: Transaction Publishers, 1999.

Carter, Patricia. "Completely Discouraged: Women Teachers' Resistance in the Bureau of Indian Affairs Schools, 1900-1910." *Journal of Women's Studies* 15, no. 3 (1995): 53-86.

Cash, Joseph and Herbert T. Hoover, eds. *To Be an Indian: An Oral History*. New York: Holt, Rinehart and Winston, 1971.

Chalcraft, Edwin L. Cary C. Collins, ed., *Assimilation's Agent: My Life as a Superintendent in the Indian Boarding School System*. Lincoln: University of Nebraska Press, 2004.

Champagne, Duane and Jay Strauss, eds. *Native American Studies in Higher Education: Models for Collaboration between Universities and Indigenous Nations*. Walnut Creek, CA: Altamira Press, 2002.

Champagne, Duane. *The Native North American Almanac*. Detroit: Gale Research, 1994).

Child, Brenda. *Boarding School Seasons: American Indian Families, 1900-1940*. Lincoln: University of Nebraska Press, 2000.

Churchill, Ward. *Kill the Indian, Save the Man: The Genocidal Impact of American Indian Residential Schools*. San Francisco: City Lights, 2004.

Clemmer, Richard O. *Roads in the Sky: The Hopi Indians in a Century of Change*. Boulder, CO: Westview Press, 1995.

Coleman, Michael C. *American Indian Children at School, 1850-1930*. Jackson: University Press of Mississippi, 1993.

Collins, Cary C. "The Broken Crucible of Assimilation: Forest Grove Indian School and the Origins of Off-Reservation Boarding Schools in the West." *Oregon Historical Quarterly*, 101, no. 4 (Winter 2000): 466-507.

Davis, Mike. *City of Quartz: Excavating the Future in Los Angeles*. London: Verso, 1990.

DeJong, David. *Promises of the Past: A History of Indian Education in the United States*. Golden, CO: Fulcrum, 1993.

------. "Unless They are Kept Alive: Federal Indian Schools and Student Health." *American Indian Quarterly* 31, No. 2 (2007): 256-82.

Deloria, Philip J. *Indians in Unexpected Places*. Lawrence: University Press of Kansas, 2004.

Deloria Jr., Vine, and Daniel Wildcat. *Power and Place: Indian Education in America*. Golden, CO: Fulcrum, 2001.

Deverell, William. *Whitewashed Adobe: The Rise of Los Angeles and the Remaking of Its Mexican Past*. Berkeley and Los Angeles: University of California Press, 2004.

Dippie, Brian W. *The Vanishing Indian: White Attitudes and U.S. Indian Policy*. Middletown: Wesleyan University Press, 1982.

Eastman, Elaine Goodale. *Pratt: The Red Man's Moses*. Norman: University of Oklahoma Press, 1935.

Ellis, Clyde. *To Change Them Forever: Indian Education at the Rainy Mountain Boarding School, 1893-1920*. Norman: University of Oklahoma Press, 1996.

------. "We Had a Lot of Fun, Of Course, But That Wasn't the School Part: Life at the Rainy Mountain Boarding School, 1893-1920." In *Boarding School Blues: Revisiting American Indian Educational Experiences*, eds. Clifford E. Trafzer, Jean A. Keller, and Lorene Sisquoc, 65-98. Lincoln: University of Nebraska Press, 2006.

Emmerich, Lisa. "Civilization and Transculturation: The Field Matron Program and Cross-Cultural Contact." *American Indian Culture and Research Journal* 15 (1991): 33-47.

Fear-Segal, Jacqueline. *White Man's Club: Schools, Race, and the Struggle of Indian Acculturation*. Lincoln: University of Nebraska Press, 2007.

Fixico, Donald L. *The Urban Indian Experience in America*. Albuquerque: University of New Mexico Press, 2000.

Fogelson, Robert M. *The Fragmented Metropolis: Los Angeles, 1850-1930*. Berkeley and Los Angeles: University of California Press, 1993.

Fortunate Eagle, Adam. *Pipestone: My Life in an Indian Boarding School*. Norman: University of Oklahoma Press, 2010.

Garcia, Matt. *A World of Its Own: Race, Labor, and Citrus in the Making of Greater Los Angeles, 1900-1970*. Chapel Hill: University of North Carolina Press, 2001.

Garrod, Andrew and Colleen Larimore. *First Person, First Peoples: Native American Graduates Tell Their Life Stories*. Ithaca: Cornell University Press, 1997.

Gonzalez, Nathan. "Riverside, Tourism, and the Indian: Frank A. Miller and the Creation of Sherman Institute." *Southern California Quarterly* 84 (Fall/Winter 2002): 193-222.

Haas, Lisbeth. *Conquests and Historical Identities in California, 1769-1936*. Berkeley and Los Angeles: University of California Press, 1995.

Hackel, Steven. Junípero Serra: California's Founding Father (New York: Hill and Wang, 2013).

Hagan, William T. *The Indian Rights Association: The Herbert Welsh Years*. Tucson: University of Arizona Press, 1985.

------. *Theodore Roosevelt and Six Friends of the Indian*. Norman: University of Oklahoma Press, 1997.

Hanks, Richard A. *"This War is For A Whole Life:" The Culture of Resistance among Southern California Indians, 1850-1966*. Banning, CA: Ushkana Press, 2012.

Harmon, Alexandra. *Rich Indians: Native People and the Problem of Wealth in American History*. Chapel Hill: University of North Carolina Press, 2010.

Haskins, Victoria K. *Matrons and Maids: Regulating Indian Domestic Service in Tucson, 1914-1934*. Tucson: University of Arizona Press, 2012.

Hendrick, Irving G. "Federal Policy Affecting the Education of Indians in California, 1849-1934." *History of Education Quarterly* 16, no. 2 (Summer, 1976): 431-57.

Herzberg, Hazel W. *The Search for an American Indian Identity: Modern Pan-Indian Movements*. Syracuse: Syracuse University Press, 1971.

Hewes, Dorothy. "Those First Good Years of Indian Education: 1894-1898." *American Indian Culture and Research Journal* 5, no. 2 (1981): 63-87.

Holm, Tom. *The Great Confusion in Indian Affairs: Native Americans and Whites in the Progressive Era*. Austin: University of Texas Press, 2005.

Horne, Esther Burnett and Sally McBeth. *Essie's Story: The Life and Legacy of a Shoshone Teacher*. Lincoln: University of Nebraska Press, 1998.

Hoxie, Frederick E. *A Final Promise: The Campaign to Assimilate the Indians, 1880-1920*. Lincoln: University of Nebraska Press, 1984.

------. ed. Encyclopedia of North American Indians: Native American History, Culture, and Life from Paleo-Indians to the Present. Boston: Houghton Mifflin, 1996.

Institute for Government Research. Lewis Meriam. *The Problem of Indian Administration*. Baltimore: Johns Hopkins University Press, 1928.

Iverson, Peter. *Dine: A History of the Navajos*. Albuquerque: University of New Mexico Press, 2002.

Jacobs, Margaret. "Diverted Mothering among American Indian Domestic Servants, 1920-1940." In *Indigenous Women and Work: From Labor to Activism*, ed. Carol Williams, 179-92. Urbana: University of Illinois Press, 2012.

------. *White Mother to a Dark Race: Settler Colonialism, Maternalism, and the Removal of Indigenous Children in the American West and Australia, 1880-1940*. Lincoln: University of Nebraska Press, 2009.

Johnston, Basil. *Indian School Days*. Norman: University of Oklahoma Press, 1988.

Karier, Clarence, ed. *Shaping the American Educational State, 1900 to the Present*. New York: Free Press, 1985.

Katanski, Amelia. *Learning to Write 'Indian': The Boarding School Experience and American Indian Literature*. Norman: University of Oklahoma Press, 2005.

Katz, Michael B. *Class, Bureaucracy, and the Schools: The Illusion of Educational Change*. New York: Praeger Publishers, 1975.

Keller, Jean A. *Empty Beds: Indian Health at Sherman Institute, 1902-1922*. East Lansing: Michigan State University Press, 2002.

Kelly, Lawrence C. *The Assault on Assimilation: John Collier and the Origins of Indian Policy Reform*. Albuquerque: University of New Mexico Press, 1983.

Knack, Martha C. "Philene T. Hall, Bureau of Indian Affairs Field Matron: Planned Culture Change of Washakie Shoshone Women." *Prologue* 22 (Summer 1990): 151-67.

Kropp, Phoebe. *California Vieja: Culture and Memory in a Modern American Place*. Berkeley and Los Angeles: University of California Press, 2006.

Lawrence, Adrea. *Lessons from an Indian Day School: Negotiating Colonization in Northern New Mexico, 1902-1907*. Lawrence: University Press of Kansas, 2011.

Lewis, David Rich. *Neither Wolf nor Dog: American Indians, Environment, and Agrarian Change*. New York: Oxford University Press, 1994.

Lindsey, Donal F. *Indians at Hampton Institute, 1877-1923*. Urbana: University of Illinois Press, 1995.

Lobo, Susan and Kurt Peters. *American Indians and the Urban Experience*. Lanham, MD: Alta Mira Press, 2001.

Lomawaima, K. Tsianina. "Estelle Reel, Superintendent of Indian Schools, 1898-1910: Politics, Curriculum, and Land." *Journal of American Indian Education* 35, no. 3 (May 1996): 5-32.

------. *They Called It Prairie Light: The Story of Chilocco Indian School*. Lincoln: University of Nebraska Press, 1994.

Lomawaima, K. Tsianina, and Teresa L. McCarty. *To Remain an Indian: Lessons in Democracy from a Century in Indian Education*. New York: Teachers College Press, 2006.

Loupe, Leleua. "Unhappy and Unhealthy: Student Bodies at Perris Indian School and Sherman Institute, 1897-1910." PhD Diss., University of California, Riverside, 2005.

McMaster, Gerald and Clifford E. Trafzer, *Native Universe: Voices of Indian America* (Washington, D. C.: National Museum of the American Indian and National Geographic, 2004).

McBeth, Sally. *Ethnic Identity and the Boarding School Experience of West-Central Oklahoma American Indians*. Washington, D.C.: University Press of America, 1983.

McCoy, Robert R. "Mission Architecture and Sherman Institute." In *The Indian School on Magnolia Avenue: Voices and Images from Sherman Institute*, eds. Clifford E. Trafzer, Matthew Sakiestewa Gilbert, and Lorene Sisquoc, eds., 35-60. Corvallis: Oregon State University Press, 2012.

McWilliams, Carey. *Southern California: An Island on the Land*. Salt Lake City: Peregrine Smith Books, 1994.

Medina, William Oscar. "Selling Indians at Sherman Institute, 1902-1922." PhD diss., University of California, Riverside, 2007.

Mihesuah, Devon. *Cultivating the Rosebuds: The Education of Women at the Cherokee Female Seminary, 1851-1909*. Urbana: University of Illinois Press, 1993.

Miller, J.R. *Shingwauk's Vision: A History of Native Residential Schools*. Toronto and London: University of Toronto Press, 1996.

Molina, Natalia. *Fit to be Citizens? Public Health and Race in Los Angeles, 1879-1939*. Berkeley and Los Angeles: University of California Press, 2006.

Qoyawayma, Polingaysi. *No Turning Back: A True Account of a Hopi Indian Girl's Struggle to Bridge the Gap between the World of Her People and the World of the White Man*. Albuquerque: The University of New Mexico Press, 1964.

Paxton, Katrina. "Learning Gender: Female Students at the Sherman Institute, 1907–1925." In *Boarding School Blues: Revisiting American Indian Educational Experiences*, eds. Clifford Trafzer, Jean Keller, and Lorene Sisquoc, 174-86. Lincoln: University of Nebraska Press, 2006.

Phillips, George Harwood. *Vineyards and Vaqueros: Indian Labor and the Economic Expansion of Southern California, 1771-1877*. Norman: Arthur H. Clarke, 2010.

Philp, Kenneth R. *John Collier's Crusade for Indian Reform, 1920-1954*. Tucson: University of Arizona Press, 1977.

Pratt, Richard Henry. *Battlefield and Classroom: Four Decades with the American Indian, 1867–1904*. New Haven: Yale University Press, 1964.

Prucha, Francis Paul. *The Churches and the Indian Schools, 1888-1912*. Lincoln: University of Nebraska Press, 1979.

Records of Sherman Institute, Record Group 75, National Archives and Records Administration, Pacific Region, Riverside, CA

Reyhner, John and Jeanne Eder. *American Indian Education: A History*. Norman: University of Oklahoma Press, 2004.

Riney, Scott. *The Rapid City Indian School, 1889-1933*. Norman: University of Oklahoma Press, 1999.

Rosenthal, Nicolas. *Reimagining Indian Country: Native American Migration and Identity in Twentieth-Century Los Angeles*. Chapel Hill: University of North Carolina Press, 2012.

Ruggles-Gere, Anne. "Indian Heart/White Man's Head: Native American Teachers in the Indian Schools, 1880-1930." *History of Education Quarterly* 1 (Summer, 2005): 38-65.

Sakiestewa Gilbert, Matthew. *Education beyond the Mesas: Hopi Students at Sherman Institute, 1902-1929*. Lincoln: University of Nebraska Press, 2010.

------. "The Hopi Followers: Chief Tewaquaptewa and Hopi Student Advancement at Sherman Institute, 1906-1909." *Journal of American Indian Education* 44, no. 2 (Fall 2005): 1-23.

------. "Hopi Footraces and American Marathons, 1912-1930." *American Quarterly* 62, no. 1 (March 2010): 77-101.

------. "'I Learned to Preach Pretty Well, and to Cuss, Too': Hopi Acceptance and Rejection of Christianity at Sherman Institute, 1906-1928." In *Eating Fire, Tasting Blood: An Anthology of the American Indian Holocaust*, ed. MariJo Moore, 78-95. New York: Thunder's Mouth Press, 2005.

------. "Marathoner Lewis Tewanima and the Continuity of Hopi Running, 1908-1912." *Western Historical Quarterly* 43 (Autumn 2012): 324-46.

Schrader, Robert Fay. *The Indian Arts and Crafts Board: An Aspect of New Deal Indian Policy*. Albuquerque: University of New Mexico Press, 1983.

Shaw, Anna Moore. *A Pima Past*. Tucson: University of Arizona Press, 1974.

Scott, James C. *Weapons of the Weak: Everyday forms of Peasant Resistance*. New Haven and London: Yale University Press, 1985.

Sherman Institute Collection, Sherman Indian Museum, Riverside, CA

Simonsen, Jane E. *Making Home Work: Domesticity and Native American Assimilation in the American West, 1860-1919*. Chapel Hill: University of North Carolina Press, 2006.

Spack, Ruth. *America's Second Tongue: American Indian Education and Ownership of English, 1860-1900*. Lincoln: University of Nebraska Press, 2002.

Spring, Joel. *The American School, 1642-1985: Varieties of Historical Interpretation of the Foundations and Development of American Education*. New York: Longman, 1986.

Szasz, Margaret Connell. *Education and the American Indian: The Road to Self-Determination Since 1928*. Albuquerque: University of New Mexico Press, 1999.

------. *Indian Education in the American Colonies, 1607-1783*. Albuquerque: University of New Mexico Press, 1988.

Talayesva, Don, with Leo W. Simmons, ed. *Sun Chief: The Autobiography of a Hopi Indian*. Ed. Leo Simmons. New Haven: Yale University Press, 1942.

Thomas, Robin Catherine. "Bringing Them Home: Native American Students from Lake and Mendocino Counties at Sherman Institute and Their Families and Peoples, 1904-1948." PhD diss., University of California, Davis, 2013.

Thrush, Coll. *Native Seattle: Histories from the Crossing-Over Place*. Seattle: University of Washington Press, 2008.

Trafzer, Clifford E. *As Long as the Grass Shall Grow and Rivers Flow: A History of Native Americans*. Fort Worth: Harcourt College Publishers, 2000.

Trafzer, Clifford E. *The People of San Manuel* (Highland: San Manuel Band of Serrano Indians, 2002).

Trafzer, Clifford E., Jean Keller, and Lorene Sisquoc, eds. *Boarding School Blues: Revisiting American Indian Educational Experiences*. Lincoln: University of Nebraska Press, 2006.

Trafzer, Clifford E., Matthew Sakiestewa Gilbert, and Lorene Sisquoc, eds. *The Indian School on Magnolia Avenue: Voices and Images from Sherman Institute*. Corvallis: Oregon State University Press, 2012.

Trafzer, Clifford E. and Patricia Dixon. "The Place of American Indian Boarding Schools in Contemporary Society." In *Boarding School Blues: Revisiting American Indian Educational Experiences*, eds. Clifford E. Trafzer, Jean A. Keller, and Lorene Sisquoc, 232-42. Lincoln: University of Nebraska Press, 2006.

Trennert, Robert. "Corporal Punishment and the Politics of Indian Reform." *History of Education Quarterly* 29 (Winter 1989): 595-617.

------. "From Carlisle to Phoenix: The Rise and Fall of the Outing System, 1878-1930." *Pacific Historical Review* 52 (Summer 1983): 267-91.

------. "Selling Indian Education at World's Fairs and Expositions, 1893-1904." *American Indian Quarterly* 11, no. 3 (Summer 1987): 203-220.

------. "Superwomen in Indian Country: USIS Field Nurses in Arizona and New Mexico, 1928-1940." *Journal of Arizona History* 41 (Spring, 2000): 31-56.

------. *The Phoenix Indian School: Forced Assimilation in Arizona, 1891-1935*. Norman: University of Oklahoma Press, 1988).

------. "Victorian Morality and the Supervision of Indian Women Working in Phoenix, 1906-1930." *Journal of Social History* 22 (1988): 113-28.

Trouillot, Michel-Rolph. *Silencing the Past: Power and the Production of History*. Boston: Beacon, 1995.

Troutman, John W. *Indian Blues: American Indians and the Politics of Music, 1879-1934*. Norman: University of Oklahoma Press, 2009.

Tyack, David B. *The One Best System: A History of American Urban Education*. Cambridge: Harvard University Press, 1974.

Udall, Louise. Me and Mine: *The Life Story of Helen Sekaquaptewa as Told to Louise Udall*. Tucson: University of Arizona Press, 1969.

Whalen, Kevin. "Beyond School Walls: Labor, Mobility, and Indian Education in Southern California, 1900-1940." Book manuscript under review by the University of Washington Press.

------. "Beyond School Walls: Race, Labor, and Indian Education in Southern California, 1902-1940." Ph. D. Diss., University of California, Riverside, 2014.

------. "Labored Learning: The Outing System at Sherman Institute, 1902-1930." *American Indian Culture and Research Journal* 36, no. 1 (2012): 151-75.

------. *Native Students at Work: American Indian Labor at Sherman Institutes's Outing Program*. Seattle: University of Washington Press, 2016.

Wiebe, Robert H. *The Search for Order, 1877-1920*. New York: Hill and Wang, 1967.

Willard, William. "Outing, Relocation, and Employment Assistance: The Impact of Federal Indian Population Dispersal Programs." *Wicazo Sa Review* 12, no. 1 (Spring 1997): 29-46.

Woolford, Andrew. *This Benevolent Experiment: Indigenous Boarding Schools, Genocide, and Redress in Canada and the United States*. Lincoln: University of Nebraska Press, 2015.

Vuckovic, Myriam. *Voices from Haskell: Indian Students between Two Worlds, 1884-1928*. Lawrence: University Press of Kansas, 2008.